THREE LIVES is Lobsang Rampa's
eighteenth book. To it he has brought all
the wealth of learning and wisdom that his
long life on earth has given him. It is a book
that his many readers throughout the world
will welcome as warmly as they have his
previous works.

D1513195

Also by T. Lobsang Rampa

and published by CORGI BOOKS

Three Lives

T. Lobsang Rampa

CORGI BOOKS
A DIVISION OF TRANSWORLD PUBLISHERS LTD

THREE LIVES

A CORGI BOOK 0 552 10707 7

First publication in Great Britain

PRINTING HISTORY
Corgi edition published 1977

This book is set in Plantin 10 pt. solid

Corgi Books are published by Transworld Publishers Ltd.,
Century House, 61–63 Uxbridge Road, Ealing, London, W5 5SA

Made and printed in Great Britain by
Richard Clay (The Chaucer Press), Ltd., Bungay Suffolk.

To my friends Eric Tetley
and
Tetley Tea Bags Cat

FOREWORD

This book is NOT presented to you as fiction for a very special reason; it is NOT fiction!

Of course, we can readily agree that some of the words in the book about life on this world are 'artistic license', but accept my statement that EVERYTHING about the life on 'The Other Side' is definitely true.

Some people are born with great musical talent; some people are born with great artistic talent, they can paint and captivate the world. Other people may be highly gifted through their own hard work and assiduous devotion to study.

I have little in the material side of this world—no car, no television, no this and no that—and for twenty-four hours a day I am confined to bed because, for one thing, I am paraplegic—no use in the legs. This has given me great opportunity for increasing talents or abilities which were granted to me at birth.

I can do everything I write about in any of my books—except walk! I have the ability to do astral travel and because of my studies and, I suppose, because of a peculiar quirk in my make-up, I am able to astral travel to other planes of existence.

The characters in this book are people who have lived and died on this world, and because of special provisions I have been able to follow their 'Flights into the Unknown'.

Everything in this book about the After Life is utterly true, therefore I will not label the book as fiction.

Lobsang Rampa

THREE LIVES

CHAPTER ONE

'Who is that old geezer?'

Leonides Manuel Molygruber slowly straightened up and looked at the questioner. 'Eh?' he said.

'I asked you, who is that old geezer?'

Molygruber looked down the road to where an electrically propelled wheelchair was just going into a building. 'Oh him!' said Molygruber expertly expectorating upon the shoe of a passing man. 'He's a guy that lives around here, writes books or something, does a lot of stuff about ghosts and funny things, and then he does a lot of writing about people being alive when they're dead.' He snorted with superior knowledge and said, 'That's all rot you know, not a bit of sense in that rubbish. When you're dead you're dead, that's what I always say. You get them there priests come along and they say you've got to do a prayer or two and then perhaps if you say the right words you'll be saved and you'll go to Heaven, and if you don't you'll go to Hell. Then you get the Salvation Army come along, they make a hell of a racket of a Friday night, and then fellows the likes of me have got to come along with our little barrows and sweep up after them. They're there yelling and banging their tamborines or whatever you call the things, shoving them under the noses of passers-by, screeching out they want money for the work of God.' He looked about him and blew his nose on the sidewalk. Then he turned to his questioner again and said, 'God? He never done nothing for me— never—I got my own bit of the sidewalk here which I've got

11

to keep clean, I brushes and I brushes and I brushes, and then I takes two boards and I picks up the stuff and I puts it in me barrow, and every so often we get a car come along—we call 'em cars but they're really trucks, you know—and they comes and they takes me barrow and they upends it with all the stuff inside and all the stuff is taken away and I've got to start all over again. It's a never ending job, day after day, no stopping. You never know what Council man is coming by in his big flash Cadillac and if we ain't bent over our brooms all the time, well, I guess they go along to somebody in the Council and that somebody makes a racket with my Boss, and my Boss comes down and makes a racket on me. He tells me never mind if I don't do any work, the tax payer will never know, but make a show of working, you get your back down to it.'

Molygruber looked about him a bit more and gave a tentative push at his broom, then he wiped his nose with a horrid sound on his right sleeve and said, 'You're asking the time, mister, if anybody says what are you saying to that there cleaner, but what I'm saying is this; no God ever came down here and done me brushing for me, me wot's having my back breaking with bending over all the day long and pushing all the dirt that people drops around. You'd never believe what I get down in my patch, pantyhose and other things wot goes in pantyhoses—everything—you'd never believe what I finds on these street corners. But, as I was saying, no God ever came down here and pushed my brushes for me, never picked up any of the dirt on the roads for me. It's all me poor honest self wot can't get a better job that's got to do it.'

The man making the enquiry looked sideways at Molygruber and said, 'Bit of a pessimist, aren't you? Bet you're an atheist!'

'Atheist?' said Molygruber. 'No, I'm no atheist, me mother was Spanish, me father was Russian, and I was born in Toronto. I dunno what that makes me but I still ain't no atheist, don't know where the place is anyhow.'

The questioner laughed and said, 'An atheist is a man who doesn't believe in a religion, doesn't believe in anything except the present. He's here now, and he dies, and he's gone—where? No one knows but the atheist believes that when he dies his body is just like the garbage you pick up there. That's an atheist!'

Molygruber chuckled and replied, 'That's 'im! That's me! I got a new thing wot I am now, I'm an atheist and when the guys wot works with me asks me what I am I can always tell 'em, no, I'm no Russian, I'm no Spaniard, I'm an Atheist. And then they'll go away chuckling, they'll think old Molygruber got a bit of wit left in him after all.'

The questioner moved on. What's the point of wasting time talking to an old creep like this, he thought. Strange how all these street cleaners—street orderlies they call themselves now—are so ignorant, and yet they really are a fount of knowledge about people who live in the district.

He stopped suddenly and struck himself on the forehead with his open hand. 'Fool that I am!' he said, 'I was trying to find out about that fellow.' So he turned and went back to where old Molygruber was still standing in contemplation, apparently trying to emulate the statue of Venus except that he hadn't the right form, the right sex, or the right implements. A broom wasn't a very good thing to pose with, after all. The questioner went up to him and said, 'Say, you work round here, you know about people who live around here, how about this?' He showed him a five dollar bill, 'I want to know about the fellow in the wheelchair,' he said.

Molygruber's hand shot out and grabbed the five dollar bill and snatched it from the questioner's hand almost before he knew it was gone. 'Know about that old fellow?' asked Molygruber. 'Why sure I know about him. He lives down there somewhere, he goes in that alleyway and then he goes down and then he turns right, that's where he lives, been living there about two years now. Don't see him about much. He's got an illness to his terminals or something, but they say he ain't going to live much longer. He writes books, he's called Rampa, and the things he writes about, they're just plain ridiculous—life after death. He's no atheist. But they do say a lot of people reads his stuff, you can see a whole display of his books in that store down there, they

13

sells a lot of them. Funny how some people makes money so easy, just by writing out a few words, and I've got to sweat me guts out pushing this broom, ain't it?'

The questioner said, 'Can you find out just where he lives? He lives in that apartment building you say, but tell me—find out for me—WHERE DOES HE LIVE? You tell me the apartment number and I'll come back here tomorrow and if you've got the apartment number and you've got what time he comes out about then I'll give you ten dollars.'

Molygruber ruminated a bit, took off his hat and scratched his head and then pulled at the lobes of his ears. His friends would say they had never seen him do that before but Molygruber only did it when he was thinking and, as his friends would tell him, he never thought much. But he could put in a bit of effort at thinking if there was ten dollars to be made for so little work. Then he spat and said, 'Mister, you got a deal, you shake hands on it and you come here tomorrow at this very same time and I'll tell you the number of where he lives and when he comes out if he don't come out earlier. But I got a friend wot knows the caretaker there, they packs up the garbage together. The garbage comes out in those big blue things, you see. Well, my friend he'll find out for me and if you like to spring a bit more I could find out some more things for you.'

The questioner raised his eyebrows a bit and shuffled his feet, and then said, 'Well, does he send out garbage, letters, things like that?'

'Oh no, oh no,' said Molygruber. 'I know this, he's the only one in this street that got a thing wot cuts up all his papers. He learned that trick away in Ireland. Some of those press people got hold of some papers of his and he's a guy, so they say, who doesn't make the same mistake twice. He got a thing wot turns out letters which looks like strips of confetti stuff which hasn't been cut off in pieces, comes out in ribbons, I've seen it meself in green garbage bags. Can't find any garbage for you because they're very careful up there, they don't leave nothing to chance and they never turn out a thing which can be traced.'

'Okay then,' said the questioner, 'I'll be around here

tomorrow at the selfsame time and, as promised, I'll give you ten dollars if you can give me the apartment number and about what time he can be intercepted when he comes out. So long!' And with that the questioner half lifted his hand in greeting and moved on his way. Molygruber stood still, so still that one would have thought he was indeed a statue, thinking it all over, trying to work out how many pints he would get for ten dollars. And then slowly he shuffled along pushing his old barrow and making a pretense of brushing up rubbish from the road as he went.

Just then a man in black clerical dress swung around the corner and almost fell over old Molygruber's barrow. 'Hey there, hey there!' exclaimed Molygruber crossly. 'Don't you go and upset all my garbage, I've spent all the morning loading it in that barrow of mine.' The parson brushed off some specks from his jacket and looked down at old Molygruber. 'Ah, my good man,' he said. 'You are the very man who can help me. I am the new incumbent to this district and I want to go on visitations. Can you tell me of new people in this area?'

Old Molygruber put his finger and his thumb to his nostrils, bent over, and did a hearty blow, clearing his nostrils and just missing the feet of the parson who looked shocked and disgusted.

'Visitations is it?' said the old garbage man. 'I always thought that visitations were what the devil did. He visits us with visitations and then we comes out in pimples and boils and all that, or we've just paid our last cent for a pint and somebody knocks it out of our hands. That's what I thought visitations was.'

The parson looked him up and down with real distaste. 'My man, my man,' he said, 'I would surmise that you have not been inside a church for a very long time for you are singularly disrespectful to the brethren of the Cloth.' Old Molygruber looked him back straight in the eye and said, 'No, mister, I ain't no God's boy. I just been told right what I am; I'm an atheist, that's what I am.' And he smirked alarmingly as he said it. The parson shifted from foot to foot and looked about him, and then he said, 'But, my good man, you must have a religion, you must believe in God. You come to church on Sunday and I will have a sermon specially for you, one of my unfortunate brothers who has to sweep garbage for a living.'

Molygruber leaned complacently on the end of his broom and said, 'Ah now, parson, you'll never convince me that there is a God. Look at you there, you get a real packet of money, that I know, and all you do is to shoot out some words about a thing that doesn't exist. You prove to me, Mr. Parson, that there's a God, bring him here and let me shake hands with him. No God has ever done anything for me.' He stopped and fidgeted about in his pockets until he found a half-smoked cigarette, then he flicked a match out of his pocket and struck it on his thumb nail before continuing, 'My mother, she was one of those dames wot does it—you know what I mean—for money. Never did know who my father was, probably a whole gang of fellows responsible really. But I've had to fight my way since I was a little lad knee-high to a grasshopper, and nobody's never done aught for me, so don't you, from your comfortable house and your comfortable job and your great big car, preach to me about God. Come and do my job on the street first and then see what your God does for you.'

Old Molygruber snorted with rage and jerked into action with unaccustomed speed. He swept his broom onto the top of his barrow, grabbed the handles of the barrow, and almost trotted down the road. The parson looked after him with an expression of utter surprise on his face, and then he shook his head and walked off muttering, 'Good gracious me, good gracious me, what an ungodly man, what has the world come to?'

Later in the day Molygruber got huddled up close with a couple of janitors, cleaners, managers—call them what you will—of some of the apartments around. They had a habit of meeting like that and exchanging juicy bits of knowledge. In his own way Molygruber was one of the most knowledgeable men on the block; he knew everybody's movements, he knew who was going into apartments and who was coming out. So then he said to one of the men,

'Who's that old fellow in the wheelchair? Writer, ain't he?'

The caretakers turned to look at him, and one laughed out loud and said, 'Don't tell me YOU are getting interested in books, old fellow. I thought you were above all those things. Anyway, this guy is writing something about what they call "thanatology." Don't quite know what it is myself, but I did hear some backtalk about it being how you live when you die. Seems ridiculous to me but there it is. Yes, he lives up in our place.'

Molygruber rolled his cigarette in his mouth and squinted down his nose and said, 'Good apartment he got, eh? Bet it's all dolled up with the latest. Like to see inside one of those places myself.'

The caretaker smiled and said, 'Nope, you're wrong there. They live very modestly up there. You don't have to believe all he writes, mind, but I do say as how he lives what he preaches. He's looking pretty bad enough to soon be going to see the truth of this thanato-something that he writes about.'

'Where does he live? What apartment, I mean?' said Molygruber.

The caretaker looked about him and said, 'Oh, it's a very secret, secret thing. People don't get to know his number, but I know where he lives. And what do you know about it, eh?'

Molygruber said nothing and they went about their ordinary desultory conversation for a time, and then he said, 'Did you say nine-nine-o-something, his apartment?' The caretaker laughed and said, 'I know you're trying to trick me, you sly old dog, but as it's you I'll tell you what his number is. It's ——'

Just at that moment one of the garbage trucks rattled into the lane and the automatic loader came into action, and the whining noise drowned out what the caretaker was saying. But being wise where money was concerned, Molygruber picked up an empty cigarette packet and fished out a pencil saying, 'Here y'are, write it on there. I won't tell who gave it to me.' Obligingly, but rather wondering what the old cleaner was up to, the caretaker did so and passed

17

it back to Molygruber who glanced at it, touched his hand to his head, and slipped the packet in his pocket. 'I have to be going now,' said the caretaker. 'Got to push out a few of these containers, it's our turn to get cleaned out next. See you.' With that he turned and went back into the garbage room of his building. Old Molygruber walked on.

Soon the garbage truck came around and two men got out, grabbed Molygruber's barrow and lifted it up to the back of the truck. 'Get in, old fellow,' said one of the men— the driver maybe, 'and we'll drive you back to the depot.' Molygruber got in, not minding at all that he was about fifteen minutes early, and back they drove to the garbage disposal station.

'Say, you fellows,' said Molygruber, 'do you know the writer named Rampa in my beat?'

'Yes,' said one of the men. 'We collect a lot of stuff from his block, he sure does seem to spend a lot on medication. We get an awful lot of empty cartons, bottles, and the like, and I see now he's been having a lot of injections or something, he's got needles what's marked "Tuberculin." Don't know what it is but that's what they're marked. Had to stop a caretaker, a relief one, from getting in touch with the police because how come anyone would want these things? Is the old fellow taking drugs, they wondered.' The garbage collector stopped while he carefully rolled a cigarette, then when he was quite satisfied he resumed, 'Never did believe in people getting in touch with the police on wild cases. I mind a little way back, last year it was, there was a real humdinger of a fuss, a relief caretaker had found an old oxygen cylinder among the garbage and in spite of the cylinder being quite, quite empty without even a valve on it she got in touch with the police, she got in touch with the hospitals until eventually after a lot of trouble it was found there was a perfectly legal explanation. After all, people don't have oxygen cylinders unless they're ill, do they?'

They glanced up and jumped into activity. It was a minute past the hour—they were working overtime and not getting paid for it. Quickly, quickly they tore off their overalls, put on their everyday jackets, and rushed off to their cars to spend an idle time lounging around the street corners.

Next morning Molygruber was a little late getting to work. As he moved into the depot to get his barrow a man gave him a hearty greeting from the cab of an incoming truck. 'Hey, Moly,' he shouted. 'Here's something for you, you've been asking so much about the guy here's something wot he writes. Get your head into it.' And with that he tossed a paperback book at Molygruber. The title was 'I Believe'.

'I Believe,' muttered Molygruber. 'Don't give me none of that rot. When you're dead you're dead. Nobody's ever going to come along to me and say "Hi Molygruber, you done pretty well in your life, old man, here's a special throne made for you out of old garbage cans." ' But he turned the book over in his hands, fumbled through a few pages, and then shoved it into an inside pocket. 'What you doing there, Molygruber? What you stealing now?' a coarse voice asked, and out of a little office a squat, thickset man emerged, extended his hand, and said, 'Give.' Molygruber silently unbuttoned the top button of his jacket and fished out the paperback book, then passed it over. 'Hum,' said the superintendent, or foreman, or whatever he was. 'So you're going in for this type of thing now, eh? Thought you didn't believe in anything except your pints and your pay packet?'

Molygruber smiled up at the squat man who, although short, was still taller than Molygruber, and said, 'Ay, ay, Boss, you get a load of that book yourself and see if you can tell me how they make out, if there's any life after this. If I go along and I see a fishhead in the corner of one of the lanes I picks up that fishhead and nobody's ever going to tell me the fish is going to live again.' He turned and spat expressively on the floor.

The superintendent turned the book over and over in his hands and then said slowly, 'Well, you know, Molygruber, there's a lot of things about life and death, we don't understand it at all. My missus, she's real sold on this feller, she's read all his books and she swears that what he writes

19

about is the truth and nothing but. My wife's a bit of a seer, you know, she's had a few experiences and when she talks about 'em it sure scares the hell out of me. In fact, only a couple of nights ago she frightened me so much about the ghosts she claims to have met that I went out and had a drink or two and then a drink or two too many, and by the time I got home that night—well, I was afraid of my own shadow. But get on with your work, lad, get down on your beat, you're late. I won't book you this time because I've been delaying you myself, but get a move on. Make one foot get in front of the other a bit faster than usual. Git!'

So old Molygruber grabbed his barrow, made sure it was empty, made sure the brush was his, and off he ambled down the road, starting another day as a street garbage collector.

It was boring work all right. A whole bunch of school kids had come by and left their filthy litter in the gutters. Old Molygruber muttered cross imprecations as he bent down to pick up toffee papers, chocolate papers, and all the litter which 'a bunch of kids' make. But his little barrow was soon full. He stopped awhile, leaned on the end of his broom, and watched some building construction. Then tiring of that he moved on to something else. A broken down car was being towed away. Then a clock struck and Molygruber straightened up a bit, shifted the cigarette to the other side of his mouth, and moved off down to the shelter in the little park—lunch time. He liked to go in there and have his lunch away from the people who sat on the grass outside just making more litter for him.

He walked down the road pushing his barrow before him, and then reaching the little shelter he fished a key out of his pocket and unlocked the side door, and in he went. With a sigh of relief he pushed his barrow out of the way and sat down on a load of flower crates, crates in which flowers for the garden had been packed. He was just rummaging about in his 'lunch pail' for his sandwiches when a shadow fell across the doorway. He looked up and saw the man he had been hoping to see. The thought of the money greatly attracted him.

The man walked into the shelter and sat down. He said, 'Well, I have come for the information you were getting for me.' As he spoke he got out his wallet and fiddled with the notes. Old Molygruber looked at him dourly and said, 'Well, who be you, mister? We street orderlies don't just give information to anybody who comes along, you know, we got to know who we're dealing with.' With that he took a hearty bite at one of the sandwiches and squashed tomato, pips and all, came spurting out. The man sitting on the boxes opposite hastily jumped out of the way.

What could the man tell him about himself? Could he say that anyone would have known that he was an Englishman and a product of Eton even though he had been to Eton for only rather less than a week through an unfortunate mistake when, during the darkness of one night, he had mistaken the wife of one of the house masters for one of the room maids with quite disastrous consequences. So he had been expelled almost before he had arrived, thus establishing some sort of a record. But he liked to claim that he had been to Eton, and that was perfectly true!

'Who am I?' he said. 'I should have thought the whole world would know who I am. I am the representative of a most prestigious English publication, and I wanted the in-depth life story of this author. My name is Jarvie Bumble-cross.'

Old Molygruber just sat there munching away, spraying sandwich all over the place and mumbling to himself as he did so. He had a cigarette in one hand and a sandwich in the other; first he would take a bite of the sandwich, then he would take a draw at the cigarette and so on. Then he said, 'Jarvie, eh? That's a new name to me. How come?'

The man thought for a moment and then decided that there was no harm in telling this fellow. After all, he would probably never see him again. So he said, 'I belong to an old English family which goes back for many generations and many years ago my maternal great-grandmother eloped with a cabman in London. In those days cabmen were called "jarvies", and so to commemorate what was a rather unfortunate affair, male members of the family have had the

21

name of Jarvie ever since.'

Old Molygruber thought it over for a time and then said, 'So you want to write about this fellow's life, do you? Well, by what I've been hearing he's had too much written about his life. Seems to me from what the other fellows and I have heard that you pressmen are making life a misery for him and his likes. He's never done any harm to me, and look at this now—' He extended one of his sandwiches. 'Look at it, dirty newsprint all over the bread. How am I supposed to eat that? What's the good of buying these papers if you don't use an ink which stays put? Never did like the taste of newsprint.'

The man was getting crosser and crosser by the minute. He said, 'Do you want to impede the work of the mass media? Do you not know that they have a perfect right to go anywhere, to enter anywhere, and to question anyone? I was being very generous in offering you money for information. It is your duty to give it freely to a member of the press.'

Old Molygruber had a sudden flush of rage. He couldn't stick this smooth-talking Englishman who thought he was one higher than God himself, so he rose to his feet saying, 'Git you gone, mister, git yourself off—beat it—scram— mosey or I'll pack you up in my barrow and take you back to the depot for the other fellows to give a working over.' He grabbed up a leaf rake and advanced on the man who got up quickly, moved backwards and tripped over all the crates. He went down in what seemed to be a welter of arms and legs and flying wood, but he did not stay down. One look at old Molygruber's face and he was up in a flash and he did not stop running for quite a time.

Old Molygruber moved slowly around picking up crates and odd pieces of wood, mumbling irritably to himself, 'Jarvie—cab driver—whatever sort of yarn do they expect me to believe—and if he had a great-grandmother, or who-ever it was, married a cab driver then how come this fellow is such a stupid dope? Ah, for sure,' he went on, his face getting darker and darker with anger, 'it must be because he's an Englishman that he's got this manner.' He sat down again and had a go at the second lot of sandwiches, but no, he was too angry to continue so he bundled the rest of his food back into his lunch pail and went out to the park to get a drink from the tap there.

He moved about looking at the people. After all, this was his lunch time. And then around the corner of a path where they had been hidden by a tree two parsons approached. 'Ah, my good man,' said one, 'can you tell me where there are er, er, public facilities for men?' Old Molygruber, in a bad mood, said, 'Nay, there ain't none of them things here, you'll have to get off to one of them hotels and say you've got to do it in a hurry. You come from England where they have 'em in the streets. Well, we don't have 'em here, you'll have to go to a gas station or a hotel or the like.'

'How extraordinary, how extraordinary,' said one of the parsons to the other, 'some of these Canadians seem to be intensely averse to we of England.' They went on in some haste to get up to the hotel just a block further on.

Just then there were screams coming from the direction of the little lake in the centre of the garden. Molygruber turned in a hurry to see what was the excitement. He walked down the path toward the pond and saw a small child of about three floating in the water; her head kept going under the water and bobbing up again. Around the side of the little pond a group of on-lookers stood idly, no one making the slightest attempt to go to the rescue and pull the child out.

Old Molygruber could move fast sometimes. He did now. He charged forward and knocked some old woman flat on her back and another one went reeling sideways. Molygruber jumped over the little stone wall and floundered through the shallow water. As he did so his foot slipped on some slime at the bottom of the pond and he went down head first, cutting his scalp rather badly, but—he got up, scooped up the child in his hands and held her upside-down as if to pour the water out of her. Having done that, he stepped gingerly along the slippery bottom and then climbed over the wall again on to dry land. A woman came rushing toward him yelling, 'Where's her hat? Where's her hat? It was a new one I only just bought at the Bay, you'd better get it.'

Molygruber crossly thrust the child, so wet and dripping, in her mother's arms. The woman reeled back to think of her dress being spoiled by the water. Old Molygruber moved on back to his little shelter. For some time he stood there glumly with water leaking down his clothes and oozing into his shoes and overflowing out on to the floor. But then, he thought, he didn't have any clothes to change into: it would be all right though, the clothes would soon dry on him. Wearily he grabbed the handles of the barrow, moved out with it and locked the door after him.

He shivered because a cold wind had come blowing from the North, and everyone knows that a wind from the North is a cold wind indeed. Old Molygruber shivered and went to work a bit harder in an attempt to generate some warmth and so dry out his clothes.

Soon he began to perspire freely but his clothes didn't seem to be drying much. He was slopping and squelching along, and it seemed to be an absolute eternity until at last the time came for him to go back to the depot.

The other men were somewhat astonished at old Molygruber's silence. 'What's wrong with old Moly?' asked one. 'He looks as if he'd lost a dollar and found a cent, not like him to be so quiet, is it? Wonder what happened?'

His old car was hard to start and then just as he did start and was ready to drive off he found that one of his rear tyres was flat, so with a very loud curse he stopped the engine, got out, and went through the laborious task of changing his wheel. With that done he got into his car again and once more experienced great difficulty in getting the thing started. By the time he got home to his lonely room he was sick of the whole thing, sick of saving people, sick of work, sick of loneliness, sick of everything. Quickly he peeled off his clothes, mopped himself dry with an old towel, and climbed into bed without bothering to have anything more to eat.

In the night he found that he was sweating profusely. The night seemed to be endless, he was having difficulty in breathing and his body seemed to be on fire. He lay there

24

in the darkness breathing harshly and wondering whatever could be wrong with him but thinking that in the morning he would go along to the drug store and get some cough tablets or something to ease the trouble in his chest.

Morning was long acoming, but at last the red rays of the sun shone in his small window to find him still awake with a red face and a burning temperature. He tried to get up but collapsed on the floor. How long he stayed there he did not know, but eventually he was awakened to movements. He opened his eyes and looked up and found two ambulance men just lifting him on to a stretcher. 'Double pneumonia, that's what you've got, old man,' said one of the ambulance men. 'We're taking you to the General. You'll be all right.' The other said, 'Any relatives? Who do you want us to get in touch with?'

Old Molygruber closed his eyes in weariness and lapsed into a troubled sleep. He did not know when he was carried out to the ambulance, he did not know when the ambulance drove in to the hospital Emergency entrance, nor when he was carried up to a ward and put into a bed.

CHAPTER TWO

'Come on, now, come on, stick out your arm and no nonsense with you. Come on, get a move on!' The voice was commanding, shrill, and insistent. Leonides Manuel Molygruber stirred slightly and then came to a blurred awareness as his arm was roughly grasped and pulled from under the sheets. 'I don't know what you are putting up such a resistance for,' the voice said irritably, 'I've got to get some blood out of you. Now come on, no nonsense.' Old Moly-gruber opened his eyes a bit wider and peered around him. Above him on his left hand side a woman was standing scowling down at him. He turned his glance to a wire basket thing standing on the table by his bedside. The basket was something like the things milkmen carry around, he thought, but where the milkmen had bottles of milk stashed away, this basket had a lot of test tubes with cotton on the top of them. 'Well, you've returned to us, eh? Well, come on with you, you're wasting my time.' With that the woman roughly pulled up his pyjama sleeve and put something around his arm, it looked like a bit of black rubber to him. Then she tore open a little packet and took something out of that and vigorously scrubbed his skin. There was a sharp pain and he jumped, and the woman said, 'Oh damn and blast it, why can't you have your veins up properly? Now I've gone and stuck it right through.' She pulled out the needle, tightened up the torniquet around his arm and then took another jab.

Molygruber looked down bemusedly and saw a big tube —a glass test tube—attached to a needle going into his arm. As he watched, the tube filled up. Quickly, with the deftness of long practice, the woman detached that tube and put on another which also filled. Then, satisfied at last with the supply of blood, she yanked out the needle and slapped an elastoplast patch over the perforation. With a grunt she put the two tubes in her wire basket after carefully writing his name on them.

The woman moved on to another bed and her snarling, whining voice rasped the other patient's nerves. Molygruber looked about him and saw that he was in a room with five other patients. Then his sight blurred and his breath became difficult and for a time again he knew nothing.

The clattering noise disturbed him. There seemed to be the clatter of dishes and the rumble and squeak of a big trolley being pushed along. Slowly, painfully, he opened his eyes again and just outside the door of the ward—right opposite his bed—he saw a gleaming chromium contraption which seemed to be loaded with chromium-plated cabinets.

As he looked a nurse came from somewhere and started handing out little trays on which were food, each tray labelled with the name of a patient.

An orderly came over to him, looked down and said, 'Well, how do you feel now?'

Old Molygruber grunted in reply because he just felt too worn out to talk, and, as he vaguely thought to himself, surely any fool could see that he was feeling pretty sick. The orderly unhooked some things from the back of the bed and said, 'Just put your left arm out straight, I'm going to take your blood pressure.' He felt an increasing constriction around his upper arm, and then he saw the orderly with stethoscopes in his ears. In his right hand he had a rubber bulb which he was squeezing. Molygruber dozed off again and awakened once more as the pressure around his upper arm was released. 'Okay,' said the orderly, 'Dr. Phlebotum will be along soon. I believe he's just starting his rounds. See you!' The orderly moved about, going from patient to patient. 'Well, what's wrong with you, old fellow, what's wrong with your breakfast this morning, eh?' he asked one man. Molygruber saw that the man had a long pole thing beside him on which was suspended a bottle with tubes coming from it. He asked feebly, 'What's that that guy's having done?' 'Oh, that's an I.V. drip,' said the orderly, 'he's having a saline solution put into him to buck up his ideas.'

The room faded again and Molygruber could hear his own rasping breath which seemed to be echoing in a vast distance. Once again he was disturbed. He felt a hand at his throat and then he realised that his pyjama buttons were being unfastened. 'What's wrong with this fellow?' asked a male voice, and Molygruber opened his eyes and looked up. He saw what was obviously a doctor with his white coat on and above his left breast he had the words 'Dr. Phlebotum' written in embroidery stitches.

'Oh, doctor, this man was brought in and the paramedic said he had double pneumonia, so we are waiting for you to examine him.' The doctor scowled and said, 'Oh, so the paramedics are setting themselves up as diagnosticians now, eh? I'll look into that!' He bent down and applied his stethoscope to Molygruber's chest, then letting the earpiece dangle, he tapped hard with a forefinger and quickly listened-in to the sound.

'I think he'll have to go for X-ray, his lungs seem to be pretty full of fluid. See to it, will you nurse?' The doctor bent down over what was obviously Molygruber's chart and then wrote something, and went on to the next patient. Molygruber dozed.

There was the sound of voices and Molygruber opened his eyes again and looked up. There was a nurse and an orderly bringing a wheeled stretcher to the side of his bed. Somewhat roughly he was pushed to one side of the bed and the edge of the stretcher was slid under him. Then with a quick flip—'like a man landing a big fish,' he thought—he was eased on to the stretcher and the orderly quickly shoved a sheet over him, and they went trundling away down a long corridor. 'What happened to you, old fellow?' asked the orderly.

'Oh, I dunno,' said Molygruber, 'I went into cold water yesterday and didn't get a chance to dry off after, so then I got too hot and then I got too cold, and I fell down or something because when I woke up I found I was in that ward. Gee, I do get a pain in my chest, isn't anyone going to do anything for me?'

The orderly whistled through his teeth and then said, 'Oh yes, for sure, we're going to do something for you all right and you'd better believe it, we're taking you to X-ray now, aren't we? What do you think we're doing it for if we're not going to help you, eh?'

There was a clatter and a bump and the stretcher came to rest against a wall. 'There you are,' said the orderly backing off, 'they'll come and wheel you in when they're ready for you, it's been a busy day already. Looks to be one of those rush-rush-rush days, dunno what I stay in this racket for.' With that he turned and hurried off down the corridor with the glass sides. Old Molygruber just lay there for what seemed hours. All the time it was getting more and more painful to breathe. At last a door opened violently and a nurse came out pushing another stretcher. 'It's back to the ward for you,' she said to the woman on the stretcher, 'I'll leave you here and someone will collect you when they've got time.' With that she took the stretcher past old Molygruber and turned to him saying, 'Well, you're the next, I suppose, what's wrong with you?'

'Can't breathe, that's what wrong with me,' said Molygruber. The woman grabbed the stretcher and with what seemed to be unnecessary force swivelled it around, through the doorway, and into a dark, dark room. There was barely enough light to see your hand in front of your face, but Molygruber peering about could see that there were strange metal tubes and chromium pieces and wires going everywhere, and at one side of the room there was what seemed to be a cashier's desk in a cinema. The woman pushed him up against what appeared to be a table but instead of being a straight table it was curved a bit.

'What's wrong with this one?' asked a voice, and a young girl came out from behind the glass cabinet thing.

'I've got his chart here. Suspect double pneumonia. Chest X-ray, back and front.' Together the young girl and the nurse grabbed old Molygruber, pushed the stretcher tighter against the table, and with a sliding swoosh he was pushed straight on to that chromium-plated table with the curving surface.

'Ever been X-rayed before?' asked the young girl.

'No, never, dunno anything about it,' said Molygruber.

'Okay, we'll soon get you fixed,' said the girl. 'There you are, lie on your back, just do what you're told, that's all we want.' She fiddled about altering the height of a big box which seemed to be suspended on chromium tubes. She pressed buttons and there was a little light, and on to his chest she projected what seemed to be an 'X'. Then being satisfied with her adjustments she said, 'Don't move now, you stay there and when I say "breathe" you breathe deeply and hold it. Understand?'

'Yes, I understand, you tell me when to hold it, then,' said Molygruber.

The young girl turned and went away behind the cashier's

desk thing. After a moment or two she yelled out, 'All right, hold it, hoold it,' and there came a sort of hissing. Then the young girl said, 'Oookay, breathe.' She came out to the side of the table and she seemed to be opening drawers or something. Molygruber could just see that she had a big metal box in her hands, bigger than his chest. She fiddled about with the metal box and then she took another one and she slipped it under the table on which he lay. She said, 'Now, we've got to turn you over on your face.' She grabbed him and turned him over, jiggling him about so that he was exactly in the right position. Once again there came the fiddling around with that black box, once again there came the little light which projected the 'X' on him. Then, satisfied with that, she walked away to the glass cubicle place and once again came the command to—'Hold your breath. Okay, let it out.' It went on for some time. Molygruber lost count of the number of X-rays that were taken, but at last the woman came back to him and said, 'Okay, I'll just push you outside and you'll have to stay there until we see if these films have come out all right. If not we'll fetch you in again. If they have you'll be pushed back to your ward.' With that she opened the door and just pushed the stretcher out. Molygruber thought it was very much like locomotives shunting trucks, and in this hospital they seemed to have no more compunction or compassion for the patients, everything seemed to be 'slap-bang, slap-bang.'

After what seemed to be a long, long time a small girl—she looked to be about fourteen years of age—came along shuffling her feet and sniffling away as if she had a terrible head cold. Without a word to Molygruber she grabbed the end of his stretcher and pushed. The stretcher moved and with the sniffling girl as his mode of propulsion Molygruber traversed the corridor again, and eventually reached the ward whence he originally came. The girl gave the stretcher a final push and said, 'There y'are—he's all yours.' She walked off.

The stretcher rolled along a bit and ended with a bump against the far wall. No one took any notice, but eventually the orderly came and pushed the stretcher to old Molygruber's bedside, saying, 'Okay, it's all over. The doctor will be along again in about an hour. Hope you last all right 'til then.'

Molygruber was slid along on the stretcher until once again he was in his own bed. The orderly pulled the sheet up to his chin and in a leisurely manner pulled the stretcher out of the ward.

An orderly came rushing in and skidded to a stop by old Molygruber's bed: 'You pull the kid out of the water yesterday?' he asked, in what was meant to be a whisper but which sounded all around the ward.

'Yes, guess I did,' said Molygruber.

'Well, the mother is here, she demanded to see you, but we said you couldn't see her, you were too ill. She's a troublemaker.' At that moment heavy footsteps were heard and a woman come into the ward with a policeman. 'You— him there,' said the woman angrily, 'he stole my little girl's hat yesterday.' The policeman moved forward and looked sternly at Molygruber saying, 'This lady tells me that you snatched her child's hat yesterday and threw it in the water.'

'Oh, what a lie!' said the old man. 'I pulled the child out of the water and everyone else was just hanging around watching her drown. The mother did nothing at all to help her. I didn't see any hat, what do you think I done with it, eat it?'

The policeman looked around and then turned back to the old man. 'You saved the child from the water? You were the fellow I've been hearing about?'

'Yes, guess so,' was the reply.

'Well, you didn't tell me about this,' said the policeman turning to the woman, 'you didn't tell me he'd pulled your kid out of the water. What sort of a mother are you to stand by and then make such accusations against the man who saved her?' The woman stood there turning red and white with anger, then she said, 'Well, someone must have got the hat, the child hasn't got it and I haven't got it so therefore he must have had it.'

The policeman thought for a moment and then said, 'I

want to go to the nurses' station, I want to phone the Superintendent.' With that he turned and went out to the nurses' station by the elevator bank. Soon after he could be heard talking, saying a lot of 'yes, sir' and 'no, sir' and 'okay, I'll do that, sir.' Then he returned to the ward and said to the woman, 'I'm told that if you persist in this nonsense I am to charge you with effecting a public mischief, so you'd better cancel your charge or you're going to come along with me, and the superintendent is feeling mighty cross with you, I can tell you.' Without a word the woman turned and stalked out of the ward, followed a moment after by the policeman.

Old Molygruber looked absolutely sickened by all the commotion, his breath rasped even more in his throat and the orderly came to him, looked down at him, and then pressed the emergency button at the head of the bed. Soon the chief nursing sister of the floor came in to look at old Molygruber, then she hurried out. Then she could be heard telephoning to the doctor on duty.

Old Molygruber dozed off, having various vivid dreams from which he was disturbed by someone unbuttoning his pyjama jacket. 'Pull over the curtains, nurse, I want to have a look at his chest,' said a male voice. The old man looked up and saw a different doctor who, seeing that the patient was awake, said, 'You've got fluid on your lungs, fluid in your pleura. We're going to tap it to get some of the water off.' Another doctor came in, this time a woman, and a nurse wheeled a tray on wheels up to the bed. The doctor said, 'Now, can you sit up, we've got to get at your ribs.' The old man tried but—no, he was too weak. So they fixed him up by having a blanket beneath his feet and what looked like a rolled sheet going under him and tied to the head of the bed, so he was in a sitting position and not able to slip down.

The woman doctor got busy with a hypodermic and kept injecting something around the left hand side of Molygruber. She waited a few moments and then pricked him with a needle. 'No, he doesn't feel it, it's all ready,' she said as she stepped back.

A nurse was busy with a large glass jar which had a nozzle at the top and a nozzle at the bottom. She carefully fixed rubber tubing to the top and the bottom and put spring clips on them. Then as she held the thing up to the light Molygruber saw that it was full with water. When she was satisfied she hung the bottle to the side of the bed, just below the bottom of the mattress. Then she stood by with the end of the tube in her hands; the far end of the tube coming from the bottom of the bottle went to a bucket.

The doctor was busy fiddling with something, he had his back to old Molygruber, and then satisfied with the results of what he had been doing he turned around and the old man nearly fainted with shock when he saw the immense needle or tube which the doctor was handling. 'I am going to put this trochar in between your ribs, and I am going to tap off the fluid in the pleura, then when we've done that we shall give you artificial pneumothorax. That will collapse your left lung, but we've got to get the fluid off first. It won't hurt—much,' he said. With that he approached Molygruber and slowly pushed the steel tube between his ribs. The sensation was awful. The old man felt as if his ribs were caving in, he felt that with every thrust his heart was going up into his mouth. The first place was unsuccessful, so the doctor tried another, and another, until in the end, in a thoroughly bad mood at his failure, he gave a quick jab and a yellow fluid gushed out and on to the floor. 'Quick nurse, quick!' called the doctor in exasperation. 'Give me that tube.' And then he pushed the tube on to the end of the steel needle. 'This trochar seems to be quite blunt,' he remarked as he went on feeling around Molygruber's chest.

The nurse knelt beside the bed and soon after Molygruber could hear water running. The woman doctor, seeing his astonishment, said, 'Oh yes, we use this trochar in between your ribs and we insert it into a pocket of fluid in the pleura, and then when we have struck fluid we release the two clips on that bottle you saw and the weight of the water—distilled sterile water—running out draws the fluid out of your lungs by suction. We'll have you better in no time,' she said with an assurance that she by no means felt.

The old man was getting paler and paler, although goodness knows, he had little enough colour before. The doctor said, 'Here nurse, you hold this.' Then he turned away to the table again and there was the clink of metal and glass, after which he came back to the patient and with one quick movement shoved the needle in what Molygruber was sure was his heart. He thought he was going to die on the spot. For a moment he experienced intense shock, and then a feeling of heat and a tingling, and he could feel his heart beating more strongly. A little colour came back to his pinched cheeks. 'Well, that made you feel better, eh?' asked the doctor, jovial again.

'Do you think we should give him an I.V.?' said the woman doctor.

'Yes, perhaps we should. Get me the things, nurse, we'll do it now,' said the male doctor as he fiddled about with various tubes.

The nurse bustled away and returned pushing what looked to be a long pole with a crook at the end. The other end had wheels on it. She wheeled it up to Molygruber's right side and then bent and lifted a bottle on to the hook at the top of the rod. She connected some rubber tubing and gave the end to the doctor who carefully inserted another needle in Molygruber's right arm. The nurse released the spring clip and Molygruber had the peculiar sensation of something running from the tube into his veins. 'There,' said the doctor, 'we'll have you better in no time. Just keep quiet.' The old man nodded his head, and then slipped off into another doze. The doctor looked down at him and said, 'He doesn't look too good to me, we shall have to watch him.' With that the two doctors moved out of the ward leaving a nurse to do the rest of the work.

Much later, when the day began to come to a close, a nurse woke up the old man and said, 'There, there, you're looking a lot better now, it's time you had a little something to eat, isn't it?'

The old man nodded dumbly. He did not feel like food but the nurse insisted. She put a tray on the table beside his bed and said, 'Come on, I'm going to feed you, no nonsense

34

now, we've worked too hard on you to lose you now.' And with that she began to spoon food into Molygruber's mouth, hardly giving the poor fellow time to swallow before she started in with another lot.

At that moment the policeman entered the ward and pushed his way through the curtains to Molygruber's bed. 'I'm keeping the press off you,' he said. 'Those hyenas have been here trying to storm the hospital. They want headlines about "Street Cleaner Saved Child" and we've told them you are too ill to be seen. Do you want to see them?'

The old man nodded as emphatically as he could, and then mumbled, 'No, bad cess to them, can't they let a fellow die in peace?'

The policeman looked at him laughing, and said, 'Oh, you've got plenty of life left in you yet, old fellow, you'll soon be out with that barrow of yours again sweeping up after all these people. But we'll keep the press away from you. We've threatened we'll take action against them if they come here as you are so ill.' He turned and went out of the ward, and the nurse continued with her feeding until the old man thought the food would be coming out of his ears.

About an hour later the doctor came back, looked at him, and then bent down to examine the bottle beneath the bed. 'Ah!' he said, 'we seem to have got it all out from that pocket. Now we're going to pump in a little air and that will collapse the lung. You see, we put air in to the pleura and that pushes the lung inwards so you can't breathe with this one, it's got to be rested a bit. I'm going to give you oxygen as well.' He put his head out through the curtains and said, 'You fellows will all have to stop smoking, you can't smoke in here while we've got an oxygen tent going.' There was a lot of angry talk from the other patients. One said, 'Why should we have to give up our pleasure just for him? What's he done for us?' Deliberately the man lit a fresh cigarette.

The doctor went out to the nurses' station and telephoned somewhere. Soon an orderly arrived and old Molygruber in his bed and with the I.V. attachment still in place was slowly pushed out of the ward and into a private room. 'There,' said the doctor, 'now we can give you oxygen without any of those so-and-so's trying to cause a fire. You'll be all right.'

Soon the oxygen tent was put in place, and a tube was connected to the oxygen outlet in the wall of the room. Soon Molygruber felt the benefits of the oxygen, his breathing improved and he generally felt a lot better. 'We'll keep you on this all night,' said the doctor, 'and tomorrow you should be a lot better.' With that he left the room.

Once again the old man slept, this time more comfortably. But later in the evening another doctor came in, examined him carefully, and then said, 'I'm going to pull this trochar out now, we've properly dried out this particular spot. We'll have you X-rayed again in about an hour's time, and then we can decide what to do next.' He turned and went out, but then came back saying, 'Don't you have any relatives? Who do you want us to get in touch with?'

Molygruber said, 'No, don't have anybody at all in the world. I'm on my own, but I hope my old barrow will be all right.'

The doctor laughed and said, 'Oh yes, your barrow is all right. City Cleaning have taken it back to what they call the depot. Your barrow is being looked after, now we've got to look after you. Have a sleep.' Before he reached the door Molygruber was asleep, dreaming of irate mothers demanding new hats for their children, dreaming of feral press reporters swarming over his bed. He opened his eyes in some astonishment and found a night orderly was disconnecting him from the I.V. apparatus and getting ready to take him down to X-ray again.

'May I come in? I am a priest.' The voice was melancholy in the extreme. Old Molygruber opened his eyes and gazed with some confusion at the figure standing before him; a very tall, exceptionally thin man dressed all in black except for his clerical collar above which his very prominent adam's apple bobbed up and down as if trying to escape from such a scrawny throat. The face was pallid with sunken cheeks and a most prominent red nose. The priest looked down at

Molygruber and then sat on a chair beside the bed. 'I am a priest and I am studying psychology here so that I may minister to the sick in the hospital. I was trained in the Maritimes.' Molygruber frowned and, indeed, scowled, and then he said, 'Oh, I was trained in Calgary—on the city rubbish dump.'

The priest looked at him and said most earnestly, 'I am distressed beyond all measure to note that on your admittance form it was stated that you were of no known religion. Now I have come to bring God to you.'

The old man scowled more and more, and said, 'God? Why do I want to hear your pratings about God? What's God ever done for me? I was born an orphan,' he said with a remarkable disinclination to sort out what could be and what could not be. 'My mother had nothing to do with me and I didn't know who my father was, it could have been one of a hundred men I suppose. I was on my own for as long as I can remember. In the early days I was taught to pray and I prayed. Nothing ever came of it until in the end I got a job shifting garbage at the city dump.'

The priest looked down his nose and twiddled his fingers, and eventually he said, 'You are in a very perilous position with this illness which you have. Are you prepared to meet your Maker?'

Molygruber looked straight at the man and replied, 'How do I know who's my maker, it could have been any one of a hundred men, as I told you. You don't think God came down and fashioned me out of dough, do you?'

The priest looked shocked and scandalised and even more melancholy as he replied, 'You are scorning God, my brother. No good will come of this, you are scorning God. You should be prepared to meet your Maker, to meet your God, for in a short time maybe you will have to go to face God and His Judgement. Are you prepared?'

Molygruber replied truculently, 'Do you really believe all that jive about another life?'

'Of course I do, of course I do,' said the priest. 'It's written in the Bible and everyone knows that you believe what's in the Bible.'

The old man replied, 'Well, I don't. I read quite a bit when I was young, in fact I used to go to Bible Class and then I found what a phoney the whole affair was. When you're dead you're dead, that's what I say. You die and you get stuck in the ground somewhere, and if you've got any folks, which I ain't, then they comes along and they puts flowers in a jam pot and shove it on top of you. No, you'll never convince me there's another life after this. I wouldn't want one, anyhow!'

The priest rose to his feet in his agitation and paced backwards and forwards, backwards and forwards across the room until Molygruber was almost dizzy with this black form like the Angel of Death fluttering before his eyes.

'I once looked through the pages of a book by a guy wot lives near where I've been working, fellow called Rampa. He wrote a lot of crap too about living after you're dead. Well, everybody knows it's all rubbish. When you're dead you're dead, and the longer you stay dead the worse you stink. I've picked up a few stiffs in my time, drunks and the like, and after a time—phew!—you can't get near 'em.'

The priest sat down again and solemnly wagged a fore-finger at old Molygruber, and then he said with some anger, 'You will suffer for this, my man, you will suffer for this, you are taking God's name in vain, you are mocking the Holy Book. You can be sure that God will wreak His wrath upon you!'

Molygruber ruminated a moment and then he said, 'How come you guys talk about a good God, a Father God who loves all His children, shows 'em mercy, compassion, and all the rest of the stuff, and then in the next breath you say God will wreak His vengeance. How come, how can you explain that? And another thing you've got to answer, mister; your book says unless you embrace God you go to hell. Well, I don't believe in hell either, but if you are only saved if you embrace God, what about all the folks on Earth before your particular form of God? What d'you make of that, eh?'

The priest stood up again, his voice shaking with anger, his face turning red with his emotion. He shook his fist at Molygruber and said, 'Look here, my man, I am not accustomed to being spoken to by people like you. Unless you embrace the teachings of God you will be struck down dead.' He moved forward and Molygruber thought the man was going to strike him. So with a supreme effort he sat up in bed. There was a sudden terrible pain across his chest, as if his ribs were being crushed. His face turned blue and he fell back with a gasping sob and his eyes stayed half closed.

The priest turned pale, and rushed to the door. 'Quick, quick,' he squeaked, 'come quickly, come quickly, the man has died as I was speaking to him. I told him the wrath of God would strike down his godlessness.' And with that he continued his run and dashed straight into an open elevator. Blindly he stabbed out and managed to hit the 'Down' button.

A nurse put her head around the corner and said, 'What's the matter with that old creep? He's enough to give anybody a heart attack. Who was he talking to, anyway?' The orderly came around the corner from another ward and said, 'Dunno, Molygruber I suppose. Better go and see if he's all right.' Together they went in to the private room. There found Molygruber still clutching his chest. His eyes were half-open, his mouth was sagging down. The nurse moved to the emergency button and pressed it with a special code. Soon the intercom in the hospital was broadcasting for Dr. So-and-So to come in emergency to that particular floor.

'I suppose we'd better tidy him up a bit,' said the nurse, 'or the doctor will be commoting around us. Ah, here is the doctor.' The doctor came into the little room and said, 'Dear, dear, whatever has happened to this man? Look at the expression on his face. I really expected that within a few days we would have him out again. Oh well.' He moved forward and fished out his stethoscope, putting the ear-pieces in his ears. Then he unbuttoned Molygruber's pyjamas and put the bell piece to the old man's chest and listened. His right hand reached out and felt for Moly-gruber's non-existent pulse. 'Life is extinct, nurse, life is extinct. I will come out and do the death certificate, but in the meantime have him taken down to the mortuary. We must have this bed ready, we have such a shortage, such a backlog of patients.' With that he took the stethoscope out of his ears and let it dangle from his neck down. He turned, made a note on Molygruber's chart, and then left.

Together the nurse and the orderly took the bedclothes off Molygruber, pulled up his pyjama trousers and tied them, and buttoned his pyjama jacket across his chest. The nurse said, 'You get the stretcher.' The orderly went out and soon came back with the stretcher on which Molygruber had travelled from the wards to the X-ray. Together the nurse and the orderly lifted the sheets on the stretcher to reveal beneath the stretcher proper another shelf. On this they pushed Molygruber's body and strapped him in—because it was not considered good to have dead bodies dropping on the floor—and then they let the sheets fall over the sides of the stretcher concealing the body completely.

The orderly chuckled and said, 'Wouldn't some of the visitors here throw a fit if they knew that this apparently empty stretcher had got a dead body on it?' With that he pushed the stretcher out of the room and went whistling down the corridor to the elevators. He pushed 'Basement' and stood with his back to the stretcher as the elevator stopped at all floors and people got on and got off. Eventually on the ground floor no one else got on, so they went down to the basement where he pulled the stretcher out. Turning it around he went right down another corridor and rapped on a door which was quickly opened. 'Here's another one for you,' said the orderly, 'just died up there. We brought him right down, don't think there'll be an autopsy. You'd better get doing him up properly.'

'Relatives?' asked the mortuary attendant.

'Don't have none,' said the orderly. 'May have to be a Potters Field job, or as he's a city street cleaner maybe the City will pay to get him buried. Doubt it, though, they're a pretty cheap skatish lot.' With that he helped the mortuary

40

attendant move the body from the stretcher and on to a mortuary table. Snatching up the sheet which had covered the body, the orderly turned and went out whistling on his way.

CHAPTER THREE

But what happened to Leonides Manuel Molygruber? Did he go out like a light which has suddenly been switched off? Did he expire like a blown out match? No! Not at all.

Molygruber lying in his hospital bed feeling sick enough to die, was thoroughly upset by that priest. He thought how unpriestlike it was for the man to turn redder and redder in the face, and from his position lying in the bed it was very clear that the priest intended to jump at him and choke him, so Molygruber sat up suddenly in an attempt to protect himself while perhaps he could scream for help.

He sat up suddenly with a supreme effort and drew the biggest breath that he could under the circumstances. Immediately he felt a terrible rasping, wracking pain across his chest. His heart raced like the engine of a car, the gas pedal of which has been pushed hard to the floor while the car was standing in neutral. His heart raced—and stopped.

The old man felt instant panic. What was to happen to him? What was the end? Now, he thought, I am going to be snuffed out like the candle I used to snuff out as a boy at home, in the only home he had known as an orphan. The panic was terrible, he felt every nerve was on fire, he felt as if someone was trying to turn him inside out just like he imagined a rabbit must feel—if a dead rabbit could feel—

41

when its skin is being pulled off preparatory to putting the rabbit's body in a pot for cooking.

Suddenly there was the most violent earthquake, or such is what he thought it was, and old Molygruber found everything swirling. The world seemed to be composed of dots like blinding dust, like a cyclone whirling around and round. Then it felt as if someone had grabbed him and put him through a wringer or through a sausage machine. He felt just too terrible for words.

Everything grew dark. The walls of the room, or 'something', seemed to close in around him. He felt as if he were enclosed in a clammy slimy rubber tube and he was trying to wriggle his way out to safety.

Everything grew darker, blacker. He seemed to be in a long, long tube, a tube of utter blackness. But then far away in the distance in what undoubtedly was the end of the tube he saw a light, or was it a light? It was something red, something changing to bright orange like the fluorescent lifejacket he wore when street cleaning. Frantically, fighting every inch of the way, he struggled along forcing his way up the tube. He stopped for a moment to draw breath and found that he was not breathing. He listened and listened, then he couldn't hear his heart beating but there was a queer noise going on outside like the rushing of a mighty wind. Then while he remained without movement of his own volition, he seemed to be pushed up the tube and gradually he reached the top. For a time he was just stuck there, held in the end of the tube, and then there was a violent 'pop' and he was flung out of the tube like a pea out of a pea-shooter. He spun around sideways and end over end, and there was nothing, no red light, no orange light either. There was not even any blackness. There was—NOTHING!

Thoroughly frightened and feeling in a most peculiar condition he reached out with his arms, but nothing moved. It was just as if he had no arms. Panic set in once again, so he tried to kick out, kick out hard with his legs, trying to touch something. But again there was nothing, nothing at all. He could not feel any legs. He made a supreme effort to have his hands touch a part of his body but so far as he could tell he hadn't any hands, he hadn't any arms, and he couldn't sense his body. He just 'was' and that is all. A fragment of something he had heard long before came back into his consciousness. It was something referring to a dis-embodied spirit, a ghost without form, without shape, with-out being, but existing somehow, somewhere. He seemed to be in violent motion, but at the same time he seemed not to be moving at all. He felt strange pressures, then of a sudden he felt that he was in tar, hot tar.

Long ago, almost beyond the edge of his memory, he had as a small boy been hanging around while some men had been tarring a road. One of the men, perhaps not having very good sight or perhaps in a spirit of mischief, had tipped a barrow of tar from the open top of the barrel and it had fallen all over the small boy. He had been stuck, hardly able to move, and that was how it felt to him now. He felt hot, then he felt cold with fright, then he felt hot again, and all the time there was the sense of motion which wasn't motion at all because he was still, he was still with—he thought—the stillness of death.

Time went on, or did it? He did not know, all he knew was that he was there in the centre of nothingness. There was nothing around him, there was nothing to his body, no arms, no legs, and he supposed he must have a body other-wise how could he exist at all? But without hands he could not feel the body. He strained his eyes, peering, peering, peering, but there was nothing to see. It was not even dark, it was not darkness at all, it was nothingness. Again a frag-ment of thought came into his mind referring in some way to the deepest recesses of the seas of space where nothing is. He idly wondered where he had got that from, but no more thoughts on it came to him.

He existed alone in nothingness. There was nothing to see, nothing to hear, nothing to smell, nothing to touch, and even had there been something to touch it would not have helped him because he had nothing with which to touch.

Time wore on, or did it? He had no idea how long he stayed there. Time had no meaning. Nothing had meaning any more. He was just 'there', wherever 'there' was. He seemed to be a mote suspended in nothingness like a fly caught on a spider's web, but yet not like a fly for a fly is held by the spider's web. Old Molygruber was caught on nothingness which reduced him to a state of nothingness. His mind, or whatever was in place of a mind, reeled. He would have felt faint, he thought, but there was nothing there with which to feel faint.

He just 'was' a something or possibly even a nothing surrounded by nothingness. His mind, or his consciousness, or whatever it was that now remained to him, ticked over, tried to formulate thoughts, tried to originate something in place of the awful nothingness which was there. He had the thought coming to him, 'I am nothing but a nothing existing in nothingness.'

A sudden thought occurred to him like a match shining in a moonless night; some time ago he had been asked to do a little extra job for pay, a man had wanted his garage cleaned out. Old Molygruber had gone there, fished around and found a wheelbarrow and a few garden tools, and then he opened the garage door as the man had given him the key the day before. He opened the garage door and inside there was the weirdest conglomeration of rubbish old Molygruber had ever seen—a broken sofa with the springs coming out, a chair with two legs broken and moths fluttering out of the upholstery. Hung on a wall was the frame and front wheel of a bicycle. Stacked around were a number of tyres, snow tyres and worn out tyres. Then there were tools rusted out and useless. There was garbage which only very thrifty people can ever accumulate—a kerosene lamp with a cracked shade, and a venetian blind, and then in the far corner one of those stuffed forms on a wooden stand which women used to use for making dresses. He pulled it all out and carted it down to a bit of waste land, and piled it ready for a garbage collection the next day. Then he went back to the garage.

An old bath fixed in tightly beneath a tattered kitchen table lit his curiosity so he pulled at it but could not move it. Then he decided he would pull the table off the top first;

he pulled and the centre drawer fell out. It contained a few coins. Well, old Molygruber thought, it's a pity to throw them, away they could buy a hot dog or two, so he put them away in his pocket for safekeeping. A bit further back in the drawer he found an envelope with some assorted paper money of different countries. Yes, he thought, I can raise a bit on these, a money changer will soon deal with that for me. But back again to the bath. He lifted off the table and pushed it outside the garage doors, then he found a whole load of rotten awnings on top of the bath, and then a broken deck chair came to life. He pulled them all out, threw them all out of the door, and then he could pull the bath into the centre of the garage.

That old galvanised bath contained loads of books, weird books some of them were too. But Molygruber dug down until he got all the books out and piled on the floor. Then he found some paperbacks which excited something in his mind—Rampa, books by Rampa. Idly he flicked over a page or two. 'Ah,' he said to himself, 'this fellow must be a load of dromedary's droppings, he believes that life goes on and on for ever. Pah!' He dropped the books on the pile and then fished out some more books. This fellow Rampa seemed to have written an awful lot of books. Molygruber counted them and was so astonished at the number that he started all over again and recounted. Some of the books had been ruined because obviously a bottle of ink had upset and trickled over a lot of books. There was one book with a beautiful leather binding. Molygruber sighed as he picked it up, ink had soaked right into the binding, marring the leather. What a pity, he thought, he could have got a few bucks for that book just on the worth of the binding alone. But—no point in crying over spilt milk—the book was tossed out to join the others.

Right at the bottom of the bath there was another book resting in solitary splendour, saved from dirt, saved from dust, saved from paint and ink by being in a thick plastic wallet. Molygruber bent down and picked it up, pulling it out of the plastic wallet. 'You—Forever' he read. He flipped over the pages, saw there were some illustrations inside.

On some sudden impulse he slipped the book into an inside pocket before going on with his work.

Now in his peculiar state of being in nothingness he recalled some of the things in the book. When he had got home that night he had had a can of beer and a big lump of cheese which he had bought from the supermarket. Then he had put his feet up and read here and there from the book 'You—Forever.' Some of the things seemed so fantastic to him that eventually he had just flung it away into a corner of the room. Now, though, he bitterly regretted not reading more because he thought that had he done so he would have had a key to his present dilemma.

Round and round his thoughts swirled like dust motes in a vagrant breeze. What had the book said? What did the author mean when he wrote this or when he wrote that? Wonder what had happened? Molygruber recalled sourly how he had always opposed the thought of life after death.

One of the Rampa books, or was it a letter which he picked up in the garbage, suddenly came to his mind. 'Unless you believe in a thing it cannot exist.' And another, 'If a man from another planet came to this Earth, and if that man was so utterly strange to humans, it is even possible they would not be able to see him because their minds would not be able to believe or accept something which was so far out from their own points of reference.'

Molygruber thought and thought, and then he thought to himself, 'Well, I'm dead, but I'm somewhere, therefore I must exist so there must be something in this life after death business. I wish I knew what it was.' As he thought that the stickiness or the tarriness or the nothingness—the sensations were so peculiar that he could not even think what they could be, but as he thought of the possibility that he might have been wrong then he was sure that there was something near him, something that he could not see, something that he could not touch. But, he wondered, is it because he could now possibly accept that there was life after death?

Then again he had heard some strange things, the fellows up at the depot had been talking one day about some guy in a Toronto hospital. The guy was supposed to have died and got out of his body. Molygruber could not recollect exactly what it was, but it seemed to him, as far as he could remember, that a man had been very ill and had died, and had got out of his body and seen some astonishing things in another world. Then, to his rage, doctors had revived his dying or dead body and he had come back and told some newspaper reporter all about it. Molygruber suddenly felt elated, he could almost see forms about him.

Suddenly poor Molygruber sat up violently and reached out his hand to stop that confounded alarm clock. The bell was clanging as it had never clanged before—but then he remembered he was not asleep; he remembered that he could not feel his arms or his hands or his legs either, for that matter, and all about him was nothingness, nothing at all except the insistent reverberating clanging which might have been a bell but wasn't. He didn't know what it was. While he was still pondering the problem he felt himself move, move at terrific speed, incredible speed, but then again it wasn't speed at all. He was not educated enough to know about different dimensions, third dimension, fourth dimension and so on, but what was happening was that he was being moved in accordance with ancient occult laws. So he moved. We will call it moved because really it is very difficult to portray fourth dimensional things in three dimensional terms of reference, so let us say 'he moved.'

Molygruber sped along faster and faster it seemed to him, and then there was 'something' and he looked about him and saw shadowy forms, he saw things as though through smoked glass. A little time before there had been an eclipse of the sun and one of his fellow workers had handed him a piece of smoked glass and said, 'Look through that, Moly, and you'll see what's happening around the sun, but don't drop it.' As he looked the smoke gradually disappeared from the glass and he looked down into a strange room, looked with horror and increasing fright.

Before him was a large room which had many different tables, they seemed to be like hospital tables with all sorts of adjustments to them, and each table was occupied by a corpse, a naked corpse, male and female, all with the bluish

47

tinge of death. He looked and felt sicker and sicker, horrible things were happening to those corpses, tubes were being stuck in at various points and there was the ugly gurgle of fluid. There was also the rattle and chug of pumps. He looked more closely in terrified fascination and saw that some of the bodies were having blood pumped out, others were having some sort of fluid pumped in, and as the fluid went in the body turned from its horrid bluish tinge and became exaggeratedly healthy in colour.

Remorselessly Molygruber was moved on. He passed an annex or cubicle in which a young woman was sitting beside one of the tables making up the face of the female corpse. Molygruber was quite fascinated. He saw how the hair was waved, the eyebrows pencilled, and the cheeks rouged, and then the lips were given a rather too vivid red.

He moved on and shuddered as he saw another body which apparently had just come in. On the eyes which were closed there were peculiar cone-shaped metal pieces which he surmised correctly were to hold the eyelids down. And then he saw a vicious-looking needle being pushed through the bottom gum and up through the top gum. He felt decidedly sick as the man who was doing the work suddenly thrust an instrument into the corpse's left nostril and seized the point of the needle jabbing it straight through the septum, after which the thread was pulled tight to hold the jaws together and to keep the mouth shut. He felt definitely queasy, and if he could have he would have been thoroughly sick.

He moved on and then with great shock he saw a body which, with difficulty, he recognised as his own. He saw the body lying there naked on a table, scrawny, emaciated, and definitely in poor condition. He looked with disapproval at his bowed legs and knobbly knuckles. Near him was a coffin or casket, or, more accurately, just a shell.

The force moved him on, and he went through a short corridor and moved into the room. He was moving without any volition of his own. In the room he was stopped. He recognised four of his fellow workers. They were sitting down talking to a well-dressed smooth young man who had in his mind thoughts all the time of how much money he could get out of this.

'Molygruber was working for the City,' said one of his former colleagues, 'he doesn't have much money; he has a car but that isn't worth more than a hundred dollars. It's a beat up old clunker, I suppose it served him well enough, but that's all he's got. That car which would fetch about a hundred dollars, and he's got a very ancient black and white TV, now that might fetch from twenty to thirty dollars. Apart from that all his other effects—well, I don't suppose they'd fetch ten dollars which doesn't leave much room for paying for a funeral, does it?'

The smooth well-dressed young man pursed his lips and stroked his face, and then he said, 'Well, I should have thought you would raise a collection for one of your colleagues who died under such peculiar circumstances. We know that he saved a child from drowning, and for that he gave his life. Surely someone, even the City, would pay for a proper funeral?' His colleagues looked at each other, shook their heads and fiddled with their fingers, and then one said, 'Well, I dunno, the City doesn't want to pay for his funeral and set a precedent. We've been told that if anything is paid by the City this alderman and that alderman will rise up on their hind legs and bray out a lot of complaints. No, I don't think the City will help at all.'

The young man was looking impatient and trying to conceal it. After all, he was a businessman, he was used to death, dead bodies, coffins, etc., and he had to get money in order to keep going. Then he said, ostensibly as an afterthought, 'But wouldn't his Union do anything for him?'

The four former colleagues almost simultaneously shook their heads in negation. 'No,' said one, 'we've approached them but no one wants to pay out. Old Molygruber was just an ordinary sidewalk sweeper and there is no great publicity if people give to his funeral.'

The young man rose to his feet and moved to a side room. He called to the men saying, 'If you come in here I can show you different caskets, but the cheapest we could do an interment would be two hundred and fifty dollars and that would be the very cheapest, just the cheapest wooden shell and the hearse to take it to the burial ground. Could you raise two hundred and fifty dollars?'

The men looked thoroughly embarrassed, and then one said, 'Well, yes, I guess we could, we could raise two hundred and fifty dollars but we can't give it to you now.'

'Oh no, I am not expecting you to pay now,' said the young man, 'provided you sign this Form guaranteeing payment. Otherwise, you see, we might be left bearing the expense and that, after all, is not our responsibility.'

The four colleagues looked at each other rather expressively, and then one said, 'Well, okay, I guess we can spring up to three hundred dollars but we can't go to a cent more. I'll sign the Form for up to that.'

The young man produced a pen and handed it to one of them, and he hastily signed his name and put his address. The other three men followed suit.

The young man smiled at them now he had the Guarantee Form, and he said, 'We have to be sure of these things, you know, because this person, Mr. Molygruber, is occupying space which we badly need because we have a very thriving business and we want him removed as quickly as possible, otherwise charges will be incurred.'

The men nodded to him, and one said, 'See ya,' and with that they moved out to the car which had brought them. As they drove away they were very subdued, very quiet and very thoughtful, then one said, 'Guess we shall have to get the money together pretty quick, don't want to think of old Moly stuck in that place.' Another said, 'Just think, poor old devil, he's worked for years sweeping the sidewalks, keeping his barrow in better condition than any of the others, and now he's dead after saving a life and no one wants to accept the responsibility so it's up to us to show a bit of respect for him, he wasn't a bad fellow after all. So let's see how we can get the money together. Do you know what we're going to do about the funeral?'

There was silence. None of them had given much thought to it. In the end one fellow remarked, 'Well, I suppose we shall have to get time off to see him properly put under.

50

We'd better go and see the foreman and see what he's got to say about it.'

Molygruber drifted along seeing the city that he knew so well. He seemed to be like one of those balloons that sometimes flew over Calgary advertising a car firm or other things. He drifted along and seemed to have no control on where he was going. First he seemed to emerge from the roof of the funeral home. He looked down and saw how drab the streets were, how drab the houses were, how much they were in need of a coat of paint, he said 'a lick' of paint. He saw the old cars parked in driveways and at the roadside, and then moved on downtown and felt quite a twinge as he looked down at his old familiar haunt and found a stranger there, a stranger wearing his plastic helmet, pushing his barrow, and probably wearing what had been his fluorescent red safety jacket. He looked down at the man languidly pushing the broom along in the gutters and every so often reaching for the two boards which he had held in his hands to lift up garbage and deposit it in his barrow. His barrow, too, looked rather drab; it was not as well kept as when he had had it, he thought. He drifted on looking down with a critical and condemnatory eye at the litter in the streets. He looked at a new building site and saw the excavated soil being lifted up and driven across the city by strong breezes which were blowing.

Something impelled him up to the Sanitation Depot. He found himself floating over the city, he found himself dipping down over a sanitation truck which was going to collect the barrows and the men. But he went on, went on to the depot and sank down through the roof. There he found his four former associates talking to the foreman: 'Well, we can't just leave him there,' said one of the men, 'it's a pretty awful thought that he ain't got enough money to get in the ground properly and nobody else is going to do a thing about it.' The foreman said, 'Why don't we take a collection? It's pay day, if we ask each of the men if they'll only give ten dollars each we can get him buried proper with a few flowers and things like that. I've known him since he was a lad, he's never had anything, sometimes I've thought he

51

wasn't quite right in his head but he always did his job although a bit slower than most others. Yes, that's what we'll do, we'll put a notice up above the paying-out booth asking everyone to give at least ten dollars.'

One of the associates said, 'How much will you give?'

The foreman pursed his lips and screwed up his face, and then fumbled in his pocket. He produced his battered old wallet and looked inside. 'There,' he said, 'that's all I have in the world until I get my pay, twenty bucks. I'll give twenty bucks.'

One of the men rummaged around and found amid the garbage a suitable box, a cardboard box. He cut a slot in the middle and said, 'There, that's our collection box. We'll put that in front of the paying-out booth together with a notice. We'll go in and get one of the clerks to write a notice for us now before the others get paid.'

Soon the men came in from their rounds. The barrows were unloaded from the trucks, the men parked them in their allotted places and put their brooms in the racks ready for the next day, and then chattering away idly as men and women will when in a throng they moved to the booth to be paid. 'What's this?' asked one.

'Our late colleague, Molygruber, there isn't enough money to pay for his funeral. How come you guys don't fork out ten dollars each at least? He was one of our own fellows, you know, and he's been on the council staff a long, long time.'

The men grumbled a bit and mumbled a bit, and then the first man moved to get his pay envelope. Every eye was upon him as he took it. He quickly stuffed it in his pocket, then at the glares around him he half-heartedly fished it out and reluctantly opened one end of the envelope. Slowly, slowly he put a finger and thumb inside and at last produced a ten dollar bill. He looked at it, and looked at it again turning it over in his hands. Then with a great big sigh he shoved it quickly through the slot in the collection box and moved away. Others collected their pay and under the watchful eye of all the men assembled took out a ten dollar bill and put it in the collection box. At last all the men had been paid, all the men save one had given ten dollars, and he had said, 'Gee no, I didn't know the guy, I've only been here this week, I don't see why you expect me to pay for a guy I've never even seen.' With that he pulled his cap more tightly on his head, marched out to his old car and drove off with a roar and a rattle.

The foreman moved to the four men who were chiefly concerned in the matter and said, 'How come you don't go and see the Top Brass? Maybe they'll give a bit. Nothing to lose, they can't fire you for it, can they?' So the four men marched into the offices of the senior officials. They were embarrassed, they shifted from foot to foot and mutely one of them held the notice and the collection box in front of one of the managers. He looked at it and sighed, and then took out ten dollars, folded it up and put it in the box. Others followed suit. Ten dollars, no more no less. At last the rounds were done and the four men went back to the foreman. He said, 'Now, you guys, we'll go in to the accountant and we'll get him to count it up for us and give us a proper statement of how much it is. That lets us off the hook.'

CHAPTER FOUR

Gertie Glubenheimer gazed gloomily around the large room. Bodies everywhere, she thought, bodies to the left of me, bodies to the right of me, bodies in front and bodies behind, what a sick, sick lot they look! She straightened up and looked at the clock at the far end of the room. Twelve thirty, she said to herself, lunch time. So she fished out her lunch pail from beneath the table on which she was working and, turning, she spread a book and her sandwiches on top of the body beside her. Gertie was an embalmer. She did up bodies in the Funeral Home so that they could be gazed at in the display rooms by admiring relatives. 'Oh gee, look at 'im. Don't Uncle Nick look good at last, eh?' people would say. Gertie was very familiar with dead bodies, so much so that she did not even bother to wash her hands before touching her food after messing about with these bodies.

A voice broke in, 'Who was the stupid idiot who left that autopsy case without filling up the chest cavity?' The little man at the end of the room near the door was almost dancing with rage.

'Why boss, what's happened?' asked one man incautiously.

'What happened? I'll tell you what happened! The guy's wife leaned over him to give him a fond kiss of farewell and there was only a piece of newspaper under the sheet, and her elbow went right through into his chest cavity. Now she's having hysterics fit to bust. She's threatening to sue us to our back teeth.'

There was a subdued chuckle around the room because things like that were always happening and no one took such cases too seriously. When it got down to brass tacks the relatives would not like it to be known that they had got their elbows inside their dearest just preparatory to interment.

The boss looked up and came trotting towards Gertie: 'Get your lunch pail off his face,' he roared, 'you just bend his nose and we'll never be able to do him up.'

Gertie sniffed and said, 'Okay boss, okay, keep calm, this fellow is a poorey, he's not going on display!'

The boss looked at the number on the table and consulted a list he was carrying saying, 'Oh him, yes, they can't go above three hundred dollars, we'll just box him up and send him off. What are we going to do about clothes?'

The girl looked to where the naked body was beside her and asked, 'What's wrong with the clothes he had on when he came in?'

The boss said, 'They were hardly good enough to put in

the garbage can. Anyway, they've shrunk so much after being washed that they won't go on now.'

Gertie said, 'Well, how about those old curtains we took down and we decided they were too faded to put up again, couldn't we wrap him in one of those?'

The boss glowered at her and replied, 'They're worth ten dollars, who's going to pay ten dollars for it? I think the best thing to do is to put some shavings in the casket, dump him in, and put some more shavings on top. That's good enough, nobody's going to see him anyhow. Do that.' He stamped off and Gertie resumed her lunch.

Over it all hovered Molygruber in his astral form, unseen, unheard, but seeing and hearing all. He was sickened at the way his body was being treated but some strange power held him there, he could not move, he could not shift from the spot at all. He watched everything going on, watched some bodies being clothed in absolutely wonderful dresses—the women—and men being done up in what seemed to be evening dress or formals, while he, he thought, would be lucky to get a handful or two of shavings.

'What you reading, Bert?' somebody called out. A young man with a paperback book in one hand and a hamburger in the other looked up suddenly and waved the book at the questioner: 'I Believe,' he answered. 'It's a darn good book, I'm telling you, it's by that fellow Rampa who lives in the city. I've read all his books and one thing's stuck in my mind ever since. It is that you've got to believe something because if you don't believe in anything you're stuck good and fast in the wilderness. Look at that fellow there,' he gestured towards the body of old Molygruber lying cold, still and naked on the table, 'that fellow is a complete atheist. Wonder what he's doing now? Can't be in heaven because he doesn't believe in it, can't be in hell because he doesn't believe in that either. Must be stuck between worlds. This fellow Rampa always says that you don't have to believe what he says but believe in something, or at least keep an open mind because if you don't keep an open mind then helpers, or whatever they are on the Other Side, can't keep in touch with you, can't help you. And somewhere in one of his books he says that when you pass over you get stuck in nothingness.' He laughed, and then went on, 'He also says that when people get to the stage just out of the body they see what they expect to see. That must be a sight, to see all the angels fluttering about!'

A man moved across and looked at the cover on the book. 'Funny looking guy, ain't he? Wonder what that picture's meant to be?'

'Dunno,' said the book's owner. 'That's one of the things about these books, you get covers and blow me you never know what the covers mean. Never mind, it's the words inside that I buy them for.'

Old Molygruber hovered closer. Through no effort of his own he seemed to be guided to places, as the men were talking about the book he was sent to hover right over them, and it stuck in his mind, 'If you don't believe in a thing then as far as you are concerned it doesn't exist. And then what are you going to do?'

The lunch hour wore on. Some people were reading with books propped up against corpses, and Gertie had her lunch spread out on old Molygruber's body just as though he were a spare table for her convenience. At last the bell went and lunch break was over. The people cleared up the remnants of their food, balled up the paper and put it in the garbage bin. Gertie picked up a brush and brushed the crumbs off Molygruber's body. He looked down in disgust at her uncaring, unfeeling actions.

'Hey, you guys there, get that body ready immediately, toss some shavings in that shell number forty-nine and toss that fellow in on top of the shavings. Then put some more shavings on top. He shouldn't leak any, but we've got to make sure that everything is mopped up.' The boss man again. He danced in to the big room with a sheaf of papers in his hand, and then he said, 'They want the funeral to be at two-thirty this afternoon which is rushing it a bit. I must go and get changed.' He turned tail and fled.

Gertie and one of the men rolled Molygruber's body on to one side and passed loops beneath him and then moved him to the other side so they could get at the loops. Little

56

hooks were pulled up to engage in eyelets, and then the body was swung up on to what seemed to be a little railway running on rods. They pushed Molygruber's body to a side of the room where what they called a shell, which was numbered 49 in chalk, was standing ready with the lid off. The man assistant went to a big bin and took out a lot of sawdust which he poured liberally into the casket until there was about six inches of sawdust. Then Molygruber's body was lowered into the casket. The girl said, 'There, I think he should be all right, I don't think he'll leak any. I've got him tied off all right down there, and of course I've got him plugged everywhere, too. I don't think he'll leak but let's put in more sawdust instead of shavings, the old man won't know.' So they got another load of sawdust and poured it onto the body until Molygruber was covered. Then together they lifted up the lid and put it on with a slam. The man reached for a pneumatically-powered screw-driver and turned down the screws as the woman put them in the holes with her fingers. She reached out and picked up a damp rag, then carefully wiped off the number in chalk. The casket or shell was hoisted up from the trestles and moved sideways onto a wheeled trolley. A purple pall was placed over it, and the whole affair was wheeled out of the workroom into the showroom and display rooms.

There came shouting and the boss, now done up as a conventional Funeral Director in very formal clothing, black jacket, silk hat, and striped trousers, moved onto the scene. 'Push him out there, get a move on will you,' he shouted, 'the hearse is out there, the door's opened and everyone's waiting. Get a move on!' Gertie and the male assistant 'got a move on' and pushed the casket along to a ramp where there was a special loading device. It consisted of a lot of rollers in a frame extending from the ramp right on to the back of the hearse. They put the casket on the rollers and easily pushed it straight into the hearse. The driver got out of his seat and said, 'Okay doke? Okay, off we go!' The Director got in beside him, and slowly the garage doors were rolled up and the hearse moved out.

There was only one car waiting outside, a car with

Molygruber's four associates in it. They were done up in their best Sunday clothes, probably clothes which had been redeemed especially from the pawnbroker. Some of these men had the bright idea that when they were not using their Sunday clothes they would leave them with the pawnbroker because then they would have money to spend until the end of the week when they were paid, and in addition the pawnbroker always cleaned the clothes and had them neatly pressed before putting them in the 'Hold' room.

Poor Molygruber seemed to be attached to his body by invisible cords. As the casket was being pushed along, poor old Molygruber in his astral form was being dragged along, and he had no say in the matter at all. Instead he was kept about ten feet above the body, and he found himself ploughing invisibly through walls, floors and ceilings. Then at last he was moved out into the hearse, and the hearse moved out into the open. The Funeral Director leaned out of the hearse and said to the four men, 'Okay? All right then, let's go.' The hearse moved out of the Funeral Home parking lot, and the four mourners in the one car followed on behind. They had their headlights on to show that this was a funeral, and on the side of the following car there was a little triangular flag fixed from the top of the window reading 'Funeral.' That meant that it could go across traffic lights and the police would not do a thing about it. They moved on and on, through the busy streets, past children playing in school yards, and came to the long climb up to the cemetery. There the Funeral Director stopped, got out and went to the car following. 'Keep close to us,' he said, 'because at the next intersection there is always somebody trying to cut in-between and we don't want to delay things too long, and you may lose the way. We have to take third on the right and first on the left. Okay?' The man driving the other car nodded so the Funeral Director went back to the hearse. They took off again with the following car really tail-gating.

Soon they reached the gates of the cemetery. The hearse and the following car moved in and up a driveway. At the top and off to the side there was a newly dug grave with a frame over it and the pulleys on the side. The hearse moved up, turned, and backed. Two men waiting by the graveside moved toward the hearse. The driver and the Funeral Director got out, and the four of them opened the back of the hearse pulling out the coffin. They turned it and moved to the grave. The four mourners followed. 'This man was an atheist,' said the Funeral Director, 'and so there will be no service, that will save you certain expense, we will just lower him and cover him up.' The other men nodded and the coffin was eased over the top of the rollers and special web straps were put under, then slowly the coffin was lowered into the ground. The four men moved up to the open grave as one, looked down, and were quite upset, quite sad. One said, 'Poor old Molygruber, nobody in the world to care about him.' Another said, 'Well, I hope he's got somebody where he's going or where he's gone.' With that they went back to their car, backed it, turned, and slowly drove off out of the cemetery. The two men beside the Funeral Director tipped a board and a whole load of earth fell into the casket with a hollow, sickening sound. The Director said, 'Ah well, cover him up, that's that,' and moved to the hearse. The driver got in and they drove off.

Molygruber hovered above powerless to do anything, powerless to move, and he looked down and thought, 'So this is the end of life, eh? What now? Where do I go from here? I've always believed there was nothing after death, but I'm dead and there's my body and I'm here, so what am I and where am I?' With that there seemed to be a loud thrumming sound like the sound of the wind through taut telephone lines on a high hillside, and Molygruber found himself speeding into nothingness. There was nothing before him, nothing behind him, nothing at either side, neither at the front nor at the back, and he sped on unto nothingness.

Silence! Silence, nothing but silence, not a sound. He listened very, very carefully but there was no sound of a heartbeat, no sound of breathing. He held his breath, or thought he did, and then it came to him with a shock that his heart was not beating, and his lungs were not working either. From force of habit he put his hands out to feel his chest. There was a distinct impression that he had put his hands out, a very distinct impression that everything was working, but there was nothing there—nothing.

The silence grew oppressive. He shifted uneasily, but did he? He was not sure of anything any more. He tried moving a leg. Tentatively he tried to twiddle a toe, but no—nothing. No sensation of feeling, no sensation of movement, no sensation that anything WAS. He lay back—or thought he did —and tried to compose himself, tried to compose his thoughts. How do you think in the midst of nothingness when you have the impression yourself that you are nothing, that you do not even exist? But then you must exist, that is what he thought, because if he had not been existing —well—he could not think. He thought of the casket being lowered down into the hard, hard earth, the earth dried out with days and days of dryness, with no rain, with never a cloud in the sky. He thought.

As he thought there was a sudden sensation of motion. He looked, he would have said, 'over the side,' with astonishment and found that he was over his grave, but how could that be when a second ago—a second ago?—what was time, time, how could he measure time here? By habit he tried to look down at his wrist, but no, there was no watch there. There was no arm there either. There was nothingness. As he looked down all he saw was the grave. He saw with considerable astonishment and fright that there was long grass on his grave. How long does grass take to grow? There was every evidence that he had been buried well over a month ago. The grass could not have grown so quickly, could not have grown in any lesser time than a month or six weeks. Then he found his vision slipping, slipping beneath the grass, beneath the earth, he saw the earthworms burrowing and moving, he saw little beetles bustling around. His sight penetrated further and he saw the wood of the coffin. Further—he saw below the lid of the coffin, saw the mouldering, decaying mass within. Instantly he recoiled and sprang up with a soundless shriek of terror, or that was the sensation that he had. He found himself quivering, absolutely shaking in every limb, but then he recalled that he had no limbs, he had no body there so far as he could tell. He gazed about him but still there was nothing to see, no light, no dark, only the void, the void of complete emptiness. where even light could not exist. The sensation was terrible, shocking. But then how did he feel a sensation if he had no body? He lay there, or should it be existed there, trying to work out what was.

Suddenly a vagrant thought came creeping across his consciousness. 'I Believe,' the thought came. 'Rampa,' the thought came. What was it those fellows had been talking about the last time he saw them up at the Sanitation Depot? A number of street cleaners were there, a number of garbage truck drivers, too, and they were talking about life and death, and all the rest of it, a talk which had been generated by Molygruber showing a book by Lobsang Rampa.

One of the men had said, 'Well, I dunno what to believe, never did know what to believe. My religion don't help me any, doesn't give us any answers, just says you must have faith. How can you have faith when there's never any proof of anything? Any of you fellows ever had a prayer answered?' he had asked. He looked about and saw the negative shakes of his colleagues' heads. One said, 'Nope, never did, never known anyone, either, who got a prayer answered. When I was a little 'un I got taught the Bible and a thing that stuck in my mind then was all the Old Fellows, great prophets, saints and what-nots, they used to pray their fool heads off but they didn't get any answers, nothing good ever happened. I mind reading one day about the Crucifixion. It said in the Good Book that Christ uttered words on the Cross, "Lord, Lord, why hast thou forsaken me?" But He got no answer.'

There was an uneasy silence among the men as they looked down and shuffled their feet in discomfort and with unaccustomed minds they tried to think of the future. What was there after death? Anything? Do bodies just return to the earth as a putrifying mass and then as sterile bones crumbling into dust? There must be something more than this, they thought. There was a definite purpose to life and a

61

definite purpose to death. Some of them looked a bit guiltily at their fellows as they recalled strange circumstances, peculiar happenings, and events which could not be explained by anything within their consciousness.

One fellow said, 'Well, that author you've been telling us about who lives downtown, well my missus been reading his books and she's been going on to me something terrible. She said, "Jake, Jake, if you don't believe anything you've not nothing to hang on to when you're dead." She said, "If you believe that there is an afterlife then you will experience an afterlife, it's as simple as that, you've got to believe that there is an afterlife otherwise you'll float like a bubble on the wind, just drifting about almost without existence. You've got to believe, you've got to keep an open mind so you can be ready to believe if you have something to stimulate your interest when you pass over." '

There had been a long silence after that utterance. The men had looked embarrassed and fidgeted uncomfortably wondering how they could get away without appearing to run away. Molygruber thought of it all as he lay there, or stood, or sat there—he did not know which—high up in nothingness, being just a disembodied thought so far as he could tell. But then—perhaps that author was right, perhaps people had persecuted him and picked on him and given him unfavourable publicity because they did not know, because they were wrong. Perhaps that author was right, now what was it he was teaching? Molygruber strained and strained to recall the fleeting thought which had barely touched the rippling surface of his consciousness. Then it came to him. 'You must believe in SOMETHING. If you are a Catholic then you believe in a form of heaven, peopled with saints and angels. If you are a Jew you believe in a different form. If you are a follower of Islam then you have a different form again of heaven. But you must believe in something, you must keep an open mind so that even if you do not actually believe now you still have an openness in your mind so that you can be convinced. Otherwise you will float idly between worlds, between planes, float as a drifting thought, as tenuous as a thought.'

Molygruber thought and thought about it. He thought how throughout his life he had denied the existence of a God, denied the existence of a religion, thinking that all priests were money-grabbing Shylocks out to con the public with a lot of fairy tales. He thought about it. He tried to picture the old author whom he had once seen close up. He focused on his rendering of the author's face, and to his terror it seemed that the author's face was right in front of him, speaking, talking to him. 'You must believe, unless you believe SOMETHING you are just a drifting shadow without power, without motivation, and without anchor. You must believe, you must keep your mind open, you must be ready to receive help so that you may be removed from the void, from the sterile emptiness and moved on to another plane of existence.'

Again Molygruber thought, 'I wonder who's using my old barrow now?' And like a flash he saw again the streets of Calgary, saw a young fellow this time pushing along his barrow sweeping the streets, stopping every so often to have a smoke. Then he saw the old author, and he quivered with fright as he looked down and found the old author was looking up with a sort of half-smile on his lips. Then the lips formed words, 'Believe something, believe, open your mind, there are people ready to help you.'

Molygruber looked again and felt a surge of rage at the man who was using his old barrow. It was a dirty old barrow now with dirt engrained in the hinges of the lids and around the handles. The broom was worn, too, not even worn evenly but worn unevenly, at an angle, and that to him betrayed that the present user was not a man with pride in his job. He felt a surge of rage, and with that a great speed—frightening, mind-numbing speed. And yet it was all so strange, how could he feel speed when there was no feeling of motion. How could he have speed without the wind on his face? Then he shuddered with terror. Did he have a face? Was he in a place where there was wind? He did not know.

Molygruber just WAS. There was no feeling of time, hardly a feeling of being, he just WAS. His mind ticked over, just idle thoughts creeping across the screen of his mental vision. Then again he pictured the old author and almost heard the words which had not been uttered: 'You must believe in something.' With that Molygruber had a picture of his childhood, the poor, poor conditions under which he had lived. He remembered a picture in a Bible and a sentence: 'The Lord is my shepherd, I shall not want, he leadeth me——' He leadeth me. The thought beat an endless refrain in Molygruber's mind or his consciousness or whatever was left to him now, and he thought, 'I wish He'd lead me! I wish somebody would lead me!' With his thought he felt 'something,' he could not tell what it was, he had a sensation that people were near, it reminded him of when he had been sleeping in a doss house and whenever any other person came by in that big room he would be aware of it, not to the point of waking but to the point of being on guard in case they tried to steal the watch beneath his pillow or the thin wallet tucked in the small of his back.

He uttered a thought, 'Help me, help me,' and then he seemed to feel that he had feet. There was a strange tipping sensation and—yes—he had feet, bare feet, and with a sickening sensation of terror he found that his feet were on something sticky, tar maybe, he thought. He recalled a time when he was young and he had rushed out of the house barefooted, and he had walked straight into where the City roadmen had been tarring the highway. He remembered the fright, the terror—he was very young—the thought that he was stuck on the road and would never get away again. It was like that now, he was stuck, stuck in tar. And then he thought that tar was creeping up along his body, yes he could feel a body now, he had arms, hands and fingers, but he could not move them because they were stuck in tar, or if it was not tar it was something sticky, something that inhibited movement, and about him he could swear there were people and the people were watching him. He felt a surge of rage, red, red rage, almost a killing rage, and he sent out the thought, 'Okay, youse guys, what are you gaping at me for, why don't you come and give me a hand? Can't you see I'm stuck, eh?' The thought came back clear and loud, almost like some of the things he had seen on the television sets which he had watched in the windows of dealers. 'You must believe, you must believe, you must open your mind before we can help you for you are repelling us with every thought. Believe, we are here ready to help you, believe.'

He snorted and tried to run after the people who were staring at him for he was sure they were staring, but he found that his movements were just flounderings. He was stuck in tar, movements were almost imperceptible. He suddenly thought, 'Oh, my God, what's happened?' And with the thought of 'Oh my God' he had seen a light in the darkness like the sunlight creeping over the horizon at the earliest part of the morning. He looked in awe, and then again experimentally mumbled 'God—God—help me!' To his delight and surprise the light brightened and he thought that he saw a 'figure' standing on the skyline beckoning to him. But no, Molygruber was not ready yet, he just mumbled to himself, 'A strange cloud, I guess, that's what it'll be. Nobody wants to help me.' So the light darkened, the brightness on the skyline vanished and Molygruber sank more deeply into the tar or whatever it was. Time passed, endless time passed, there was no indication of how much time passed, but the entity that had been Molygruber just rested 'somewhere', immersed in the darkness of disbelief, and around him there were those who would help if only he would open his mind to belief, open his mind so that the helpers could do their task and lead him forward to the light—to whatever form of life or existence there was.

He was in considerable turmoil, worse because he could not feel arms, legs, or anything else, and it was—well, disturbing to say the least. For some reason he could not get that old author out of his mind, it was really sticking there and prodding at him. There was something bubbling beneath his consciousness. At last he got it.

A few months before he had seen the old author in the electrically propelled wheelchair. He had been tootling around in the new park which had been made, and there was a man with him. Molygruber, as was his wont, had stopped to listen to the two conversing. There was something the author was saying: 'You know, the Christian

Bible sheds a lot of light on the matter of life after death and it always strikes me as most remarkable that Christians—Catholics in particular—believe in saints, angels, devils and so on, and yet for some extraordinary reason they still seem to doubt life after death. So how are they going to explain Ecclesiastes 12:5–7 which actually says, "Because Man goes to his eternal home and the mourners go about the streets; before the silver cord is snapped or the golden bowl is broken or the pitcher is broken at the fountain or the wheel broken at the cistern, and the dust returns to the earth as it was and the spirit returns to God who gave it." Well,' the old author had said to the other man, 'you know what that means, don't you? It means that of the body of a person, one part returns to the dust from which it was alleged to have been made, and the other portion returns to God or to life beyond this. Now, that's the Christian Bible, they acknowledge life after death, but the Christians apparently do not. But then there are a lot of things Christians don't believe in. They'll find out, though, when they get to the Other Side!'

Molygruber really jumped, or rather he felt as if he jumped. How can you jump if you have no body? The words seemed as though they had been uttered just behind him. Somehow he managed to turn around his consciousness but there was nothing behind him, so he mused on the problem for a time, thinking perhaps he had been lost, perhaps he had allowed his early life to distort his thinking, perhaps there was something in the life after the earth-life. There must be, he concluded, because he had seen his body dying, he had seen his body dead, and—he had shuddered and would have been sick if he could—he had seen his body decaying with the skeleton bones showing through the rotting flesh.

Yes, he muttered to himself, if one can mutter without a voice, there must be something in life after death, he must have been misled all these years. Maybe the bitterness he had generated through hardship in his early life had distorted his values. Yes—there must be some sort of life because he was still alive, or he supposed he was, and if he was not alive how was he thinking these things? Yes, he must be having some sort of a life.

As that thought came to him he felt a most peculiar thing happening, he seemed to be prickling all over, prickling to what would have been the outline of a body. He felt that he had arms and hands, legs and feet, and as he twisted a bit he could sense them. And then—oh, glory be to goodness—the light was growing. In the nothingness, in the utter void in which he had been existing light was beginning to penetrate; it was a rosy hue, very faint at first but growing stronger. And then with a suddenness which almost made him sick he tilted and seemed to be falling, falling on his feet. After a short while he landed on something sticky, something gooey, and about him he could see a black fog interspersed with rays of pinkish light. He tried to move and found that while motion was not entirely inhibited it was difficult—difficult. He seemed to be in some viscid material which slowed him up, which made him move in slow-motion, and there he was floundering about, lifting first one foot and then the other. He thought to himself that he was like one of those weird monsters sometimes portrayed on the covers of gaudy science fiction books.

He shouted aloud, 'Oh God, if there is a God, help me!' No sooner were the words uttered than he felt a change in his circumstances. The sticky goo disappeared, the material around him became thinner, and he could faintly discern figures moving about. It was a strange, strange sensation. He likened it to being a plastic bag, the plastic being smoke coloured. He was there trying to peer out through the hazy plastic and getting nowhere.

He stood there shielding his eyes with his hands and trying to force himself to see whatever there was to see. He got an impression more than vision of people stretching out their hands to reach him but not being able to touch him, there seemed to be some barrier, some invisible transparent wall.

Oh goodness, he thought, if only this unmentionable colour would go away, if only I could tear down this wall, or paper, or plastic or whatever it is. I can't see what these people are, they may be wanting to help me, they may be wanting to kill me, but how can they do that when I am dead already? Or am I dead? He shuddered, and shuddered again as a sudden thought came to him: 'Am I in the hospital?' he said to himself. 'Am I having nightmares after seeing that priest? Maybe I am alive back on Earth and this is all a hideous nightmare. I wish I knew!'

Faintly, faintly, as though from a great distance a voice came to him, so faint, so unclear that he had to strain and strain to resolve what was being said: 'Believe, believe. Believe in life hereafter. Believe, only believe and we can set you free. Pray to God. There is a God. It doesn't matter what you call Him, it doesn't matter what form of religion, every religion has a God. Believe. Call unto your own God for help. We are waiting, waiting.'

Molygruber stood still. No more did his feet continue their ceaseless tramping to try to break through the veil that surrounded him. He stood quietly. He thought of the old author, he thought of the priests, and he rejected the priests out of hand as being nothing but fakes looking for an easy way to get a living by preying on the superstitions of others. He thought back to his early days, thought of the Bible, and then he prayed to God for enlightenment: 'Oh Mighty God, whatever form you adopt, help me, I am stuck, I am lost, I have my being but I have no being. Help me and let others help me.' With that and with a believing heart he felt a sudden shock as if he had touched two bare wires on an electric light standard. For a moment he reeled as the veil rent.

CHAPTER FIVE

The veil rent; the black surrounding Molygruber split with a jagged tear right in front of him, then he was blinded. Desperately he pushed his hands over his eyes thanking 'goodness' that now once again he had hands. The light was searing, never before had he seen such light, he thought, but then—had he? Well, he thought back to his days as a street orderly or garbage collector, he thought of the big steel buildings he had seen erected and the welding equipment, the vivid light which the act of welding produced, vivid, vivid, searing to the eyes so that the operators had to use dark glasses all the time. Molygruber pressed his eyelids shut, pressed his hands over the eyes, and still he imagined he could see that light beating in through. Then he got control of himself somewhat and very carefully and very slightly uncovered his eyes. It was bright, there was no doubt about that, the light beat in through his closed eyelids. Oh yes, it was bright all right, so he half opened his eyes making them mere slits and peered out.

My! What a wonderful scene he saw. The black had rolled away, disappeared, vanished for ever he hoped, and he was standing near trees. As he looked down he saw vivid lush green grass, he had never seen grass like that before. Then on the grass he saw little white things with yellow centres. He wracked his brain, whatever could it be? It came back to him, of course, daisies, little daisies in the fields. He had never seen them in reality before but only in pictures, and at some time or other on a T.V. programme which he had watched through a shop window. But there were more things to see than daisies. He raised his eyes and looked sideways, there were two people there, one each side, and they were smiling down at him—smiling down because Molygruber was quite a small man, one of those insignificant little weasel people, shrunken, shrivelled with gnarled hands and weatherbeaten features. So he looked up at these two people, he had never seen them before but they were smiling at him in a very kind manner indeed.

'Well, Molygruber?' said one, 'And what do you think of it here?' Molygruber stood mute, how did he know how he felt, how did he know what he thought of the place, he had hardly seen it yet. He looked at his feet and was happy to see that he had feet. Then he let his eyes travel up his body. On that instant he jumped about a foot in the air and he blushed from the roots of his hair to the nails on his toes. 'Jumping bejeepers!' he said to himself, 'and here's me standing in front of these people with nary a stitch on me to cover my nakedness!' Quickly his hands went down to the immemorial gesture of people caught with their pants off. The two men beside him roared with laughter. One said, 'Molygruber, Molygruber, what is wrong with you lad, you weren't born with clothes on, were you? If you were then you are about the only person who ever has been. If you want some clothes think them up!'

Molygruber was in quite a panic, for a moment he could not think what clothes were like he was in such a state of confusion. Then he thought of what was called a 'union suit' or 'boiler suit', a thing which was a combination garment, a suit which went from the ankles up to the neck with sleeves to it, and you put it on through an opening in the front. No sooner had he thought about it than he found he was clad in a union suit. He looked down and shuddered anew, it was a bright red union suit, the colour of a perfect blush. The two men laughed again and a woman walking on a path nearby turned toward them and smiled. As she walked toward them she called out, 'What is this Boris, a new one still afraid of his own skin?' The one called Boris laughed and replied, 'Yes, Maisie, we get them every day, don't we?'

Molygruber shuddered as he looked at the woman, he thought, 'Well, she's been a right one for sure, hope I'm safe in this, I don't know anything about women!' They all laughed uproariously. Poor Molygruber did not realise that on this particular plane of existence everyone was telepathic!

70

'Look about you, Molygruber,' said the woman, 'then we'll take you off and give you a briefing on where you are and all the rest of it. You have been a sore trial to us, you wouldn't come out of your black cloud no matter what we said to you.'

Molygruber muttered something to himself, and it was such a mutter that it even came out as a garbled mutter by telepathy. But he looked about him. He was in some sort of park, never in his life had he imagined that there would be such a park as this; the grass was greener than any grass he had ever seen before, the flowers—and there were flowers in great profusion—were of more vivid hues than anything he had ever seen. The sun was beating down, it was pleasantly warm, there was the hum of insects and the chirping of birds. Molygruber looked up, the sky was blue, an intense deep blue, with white fleecy clouds. Then Molygruber almost fell with astonishment, he felt his legs grow weak: 'Cor!' he said, 'Where's the flippin' sun?'

One of the men smiled and said, 'You are not on Earth, you know, Molygruber, you are not anywhere near Earth, you are a long, long way away in a different time, in a different plane of existence altogether. You have a lot to learn, my friend!'

'Cor!' said Molygruber, 'How in the name of tarnation can you have sunlight when there ain't no sun?'

His three companions, two men and a woman, just smiled at him and the woman took him gently by the arm saying, 'Come on, we'll take you in and then we will explain a lot of things to you.' Together the four of them walked across the grass and on to a beautifully paved path. 'Hey!' shouted Molygruber, 'This 'ere path ain't half stinging my feet, I haven't got my shoes on!'

That caused a fresh outburst of merriment. Boris said, 'Well, Molygruber, why don't you think up a pair of shoes or a pair of boots or whatever you want? You managed it with your clothing, although I must say I don't think much of the colour, you ought to change it.'

Molygruber thought and thought; he thought what a sight he must have looked dressed up in the red union suit

71

and with no shoes. He wished he was free of that wretched suit, and immediately he was! 'Ow,' he screamed, 'and now I'm nekkid in front of a female. Oh sad is me, I've never been nekkid in front of a female before. Oh cor, whatever will she think of me?'

The woman absolutely shouted with laughter and several people on the path turned to watch with amusement what was going on. The woman said, 'Well, well, well, it's quite all right, Molygruber, you haven't much to show after all, have you? But anyway just think of yourself dressed up in your Sunday best with a nice pair of shoes beautifully polished, and if you think about it you will be dressed in those things.' He did, and he was.

Molygruber walked along very gingerly, every time he looked at the woman he blushed anew, he was getting uncomfortably hot under the collar because poor old Molygruber on Earth had been one of those unfortunate people who liked to watch and not do, and that is even worse when you cannot go anywhere to watch and you cannot have anyone with whom to do it! Molygruber's knowledge of the opposite sex, incredible though it seems in this modern age, was confined to what he saw in magazines on the magazine racks of stores and the somewhat lurid pictures which were put out at the front of the local cinemas to titillate the appetites of prospective customers.

He thought again about his past, thought again how little he knew of women. He called to mind how he had thought that women were just about solid from the neck down, all the way to their knees, he had never considered how they walked under such conditions. But then he had seen some girls bathing in the river and he saw that they had legs, arms, etc., just as he had. He was roused from his thoughts by screams of laughter and he found he had collected quite a crowd, people had got his thoughts because thought and speech were much the same on this world. He looked about him, blushed anew, and really took to his heels. The two men and the woman ran after him, absolutely gasping trying to keep up with him, and falling back every so often because they laughed so much. Molygruber ran on and on, until at last his energy was spent and he sank down with a thud on a park bench. His pursuers caught up with him and they were absolutely weeping with merriment.

'Molygruber, Molygruber, you'd better keep from thinking until we get you inside.' They indicated a beautiful building just off to the right. 'Just keep your mind on keeping your clothes on until we get in that building. We will explain everything to you.'

They rose to their feet and the two men moved one each side of Molygruber and each grasped him by an arm. Together they marched on and turned off the path to the right and entered a very elegant marble entranceway. Inside it was cool and there was a pleasantly subdued light which seemed to be radiating from the walls. There was a reception desk much the same as Molygruber had seen when peering through hotel doors. A man there smiled pleasantly and said, 'New one?' Maisie nodded her head and said, 'Yes, a very green one too.' Molygruber looked down at himself in horror thinking for a moment that he had gone from red to green, and he was brought back to his senses by renewed laughter.

They moved on across the hall and down a corridor. There were a number of people about there. Molygruber kept on blushing, some of the men and women were clad in clothes of various types, some wore quite outlandish clothes, others wore nothing at all and did not seem to be perturbed in the slightest.

By the time they got Molygruber into a very comfortably furnished room he was sweating profusely, he was sweating as much as if he had just come out of a swimming pool, not that he had ever been in one. He sank into a chair with a sigh of relief and started dabbing at his face with the handkerchief which he had found in his pocket. 'Phew, phew!' quoth he. 'Let me get out of this, let me get back to Earth, I can't stick a place like this!' Maisie laughed down at him and said, 'But you have to stay here, Molygruber. Remember? You are an atheist, you do not believe in a God, you do not believe in a religion, you do not believe in life after death. Well, you are still here so there must be some life after death, mustn't there?'

There were very large windows in the room to which they had taken Molygruber. His eyes kept straying to the windows, looking in fascination to the scene outside, the beautiful, beautiful parkland and a lake in the centre with a pleasant river flowing into the lake. He saw men and women and a few children. Everyone seemed to be walking about purposefully as if they knew where they were going, as if they knew what they were going to do. He looked in utter fascination as a man suddenly swerved off a path and sat down on a park bench and took a packet of sandwiches out of his pocket! Quickly he tore off the wrappings and carefully deposited the wastepaper in a bin placed near the park bench. Then he set to to demolish the sandwiches. As he watched Molygruber felt faint, he heard horrid rumblings coming from his abdomen. He looked up at Maisie and said, 'By golly, I feel hungry, when do we eat round here?' He felt about in his pocket wondering if he had any money on him, he could have done with a hamburger or something like that. The woman looked down at him with sympathetic understanding and said, 'You can have whatever food you like, Molygruber, whatever you desire to drink also. Just think what you want and you can have it, but remember that you think up a table first or else you have to eat off the floor.'

One of the men turned toward him and said, 'We will leave you for a little time, Molygruber. You feel that you want food, well, think what you want but, as Maisie said, think of a table first. When you have had this food, which truly you don't need, we will come back to you.' With that they went to the wall, which parted; they stepped through, and the wall closed behind them.

It seemed all very peculiar to Molygruber, what was all this about thinking up your food? What was all this about not wanting food? The fellow had said he truly did not need it, what did he mean by that? However, the pangs of hunger were pressing, terribly pressing. Molygruber was so hungry that he thought he was going to faint: it was a familiar sensation, often in early years he had fainted through sheer

74

hunger and such a thing is thoroughly unpleasant.

He wondered how he had to think. First of all, though, what about this table? Well, he knew what a table was like, any fool would know that, but when he came to THINK about it it was not so easy. His first attempt at thinking up a table was ridiculous in the extreme. He thought of how he had looked in furniture shops while he was sweeping the sidewalks, he thought of a nice round metal table with a sunshade over it, and then his attention had been drawn to another decorated table like a work table for women. Now, to his astonishment, he found that the creation in front of him was a white metal table, or half of it, and half of a ladies' work table which was quite an unstable contraption. He pushed his hands at it and said, 'Phew! Go away, go away fast,' just as he had seen in some film years before. Then he thought again, and he thought of a table in the park that he used to visit, a thing made of planks and logs. He pictured it as clearly as he could and commanded it to be in front of him. Well, it was! It was a rough piece of work indeed, the planks were almost as crude as the logs themselves and he saw that he had forgotten to think up a seat, but that was all right, he could use the chair in the room. He pulled one up to the table and then found that the table he had thought into being had no relation to actual size, he could sit under it complete with the chair.

At last he got everything right, then he thought of food. Poor Molygruber was one of the world's unfortunates, he had lived 'hand to mouth' all his life, lived on coffee, soft drinks, and things like hamburgers, so he thought of a plate of hamburgers and when they materialised in front of him he grabbed one in a hurry and gave a hearty bite. The whole thing collapsed because there was nothing inside! After many trials and many errors he decided that he had to think clearly, clearly, clearly from the ground up, so to speak, and if he wanted a hamburger he had to think of the filling and then put the other pieces outside. At last he got it just right, but as he bit into the finished product he decided that there was not much taste to it. It was even worse when he tried the coffee he had thought up—it looked all right but the taste was nothing that he had ever tasted before and nothing that he ever wanted to taste again. He came to the conclusion that his imagination was wrong, but he kept on trying, producing this and then that but never going far from coffee and hamburgers and perhaps a piece of bread, but because he had never in his life eaten fresh bread it was always stale mouldy stuff.

For some time there was the sound of Molygruber's champing jaws as he devoured hamburgers, and then there was the slurping as he drank his coffee. Then he just pushed away from the table and sat back to think of all the peculiar things that had happened to him. First of all he remembered that he did not believe in life after death, where was he now then? He thought of his decaying body and the involuntary look at it, and he was almost sick all over the floor. Then he thought of the strange experiences, first he appeared to be stuck in a barrel of tar, the tar had vanished and been replaced by black smoke like the time he had had a kerosene lamp and turned it too high before leaving his room and when he got back he thought at first he had gone blind, he could not see anything at all because there were black smuts flying all over the place. He remembered what his landlady had said to him!

But suddenly he turned around. There was Boris standing beside him saying, 'Well, you've had a good meal I see, but why do you stick to these awful hamburgers? I think they are vile things. You can have whatever you want, you know, provided you think of it carefully, provided you build it up stage by stage from the ingredients up to the final cooked thing.' Molygruber looked up at him and said, 'Where do I wash up the dishes?'

Boris laughed at him in honest amusement and said, 'My dear man, you don't wash dishes here, you think up dishes and you think away dishes. All you have to do when you finish is to think of the dishes disappearing and their component parts going back into Nature's reservoir. It's simple, you'll get used to it. But you don't need to eat, you know, you get all the nourishment you need from the atmosphere.'

Molygruber felt really sour about the whole affair, how ridiculous it was to say that you got nourishment from the atmosphere around one, it was too absurd to be believed, what sort of a man did this Boris think he was? He, Molygruber, knew what it was to starve, he knew what it was to fall on to the sidewalk in a faint from lack of food, he knew what it was like to have a policeman come and kick him in the ribs and tell him to get to his feet, get gone or else!

The man said, 'Well, we've got to go, it's no good sticking here all the time, I've got to take you down to see the doctor, he's going to tell you a few things and try to help you straighten out. Come along.' With that he thought at the table and the remnants of the meal and the whole lot disappeared into thin air. Then he led Molygruber up to the wall which parted before them and opened out into a long shining corridor. People were wandering about but they all seemed to have a purpose, they all seemed to be going somewhere, all seemed to be doing something, and yet he, Molygruber, was completely befuzzled about everything.

He and the man walked down the corridor, then they turned a corner and the man knocked at a green door: 'Come in,' said a voice and the man pushed Molygruber in and turned on his tracks leaving them.

Molygruber looked about him in fright. Again it was a comfortable room but the big man sitting at a desk really frightened him, it made him think of a Medical Officer of Health he had seen before—yes, that was it, the Medical Officer of Health who had examined him when he wanted to get the job as street cleaner. The man had been very brusque and had sneered at Molygruber's poor physique and said he didn't think him strong enough to push a broom. But, anyway, he had relented enough to say that, yes, Molygruber was fit enough to do a job of cleaning the sidewalks.

But now this man sitting at his desk looked up and smiled cheerfully saying, 'Come and sit here, Moly, I've got to talk to you.' Hesitating, almost afraid to take a step, Molygruber moved forward and quite shakily sat on a chair. The big man looked him up and down and said, 'More nervous than

77

most, aren't you? What's wrong with you, lad?' Poor
Molygruber did not know what to say; life had been such a
terrible thing to him and now it seemed to him that death
was even worse, so his story poured out.

The big man sat back and listened. Then he said, 'Now
you listen to me for a bit. I know you have had a rough
time but you have made it rougher for yourself, you haven't
got a mere chip on your shoulder, you've got a log or
perhaps the whole forest. You've got to change your concep-
tions about a lot of things.' Molygruber stared at him, some
of the words meant nothing to him and the big man at last
asked, 'Well, what is it? What's wrong now?' Molygruber
replied, 'Some of the words, I just don't understand them,
I didn't get any education, you know, only learned what I
picked up by myself.'

The man thought for a moment, apparently reviewing in
his mind just what he had said. Then he said, 'Oh, I don't
think I said any unusual words, what don't you understand?'

Molygruber looked down and said humbly, 'Conception,
I always thought conception was what people did when they
were having babies starting up, that's the only meaning I
know.'

The big man, the doctor, gazed at Molygruber with open-
mouthed amazement, then he laughed and laughed and
laughed and said, 'Conception? Well, conception doesn't
mean just that, it also means understanding. If you have no
conception of a thing you have no understanding of it, and
that's all it means—you have no conception of this, that, or
something else. Let's make it simpler then, let's say you
don't know a darn thing about it, but you've got to.'

All this was a great puzzle to Molygruber, his mind was
still on conception and if the man had meant understanding
or misunderstanding or not understanding then why in the
name of old scrubbing brushes couldn't he say so? But then
he realised the man was talking so he sat back and listened.

'You did not believe in death, or rather, you did not
believe in life after death. You left your body and you
floated around, you didn't seem to get it into your thick

head that you had left a decaying body and you were still alive, you were concentrating on nothingness all the time. So if you can't imagine anywhere you can't go there, can you? If you make yourself so darn sure that there is nothing then for you, there is nothing, you only get what you expect, you only get what you believe, what you can realise, what you can understand, so we tried to shock you and that is why we pushed you back to the Funeral Home to let you see a few stiffs being parked and polished and done up for show. We tried to let you see that you were just a poor stiff with nobody to care a donkey's hoot about you, that's why you got buried in a coat of sawdust, but even that wasn't enough, we had to show you your grave, we had to show you your coffin, and then we showed you your rotting body. We didn't like it but it took even more than that to wake you up to the fact that you weren't dead.'

Molygruber sat there like a man in a trance. He was dimly understanding and trying hard to understand more. But the doctor went on, 'Matter cannot be destroyed, it can only change its form and inside a human body there is a living immortal soul, a soul that lasts for ever and ever and ever. It takes more than one body because it's got to get all manner of experiences. If it has to be fighting experience it takes the body of a warrior, and so on. But when the body is killed it is no more than having a worn out suit of clothes tossed in the garbage bin. The soul, the astral body, call it whatever you like, moves on, moves out of the wreckage, moves away from the garbage and is ready to start again. But if that soul has lost a lot of comprehension or even did not have any comprehension then we've got quite a job teaching it.'

Molygruber nodded and he was dimly thinking of that old author who had written some things which were quite beyond Molygruber's comprehension at the time, but now little bits were fitting in and fitting in and fitting in like a jigsaw puzzle nearing its completion.

The doctor said, 'If a person doesn't believe in heaven or a life hereafter, then when that person gets to the other side of death he wanders about; there is nowhere for him to go, there is no one to greet him because all the time he is thoroughly convinced that there is nothing, he is in the position of a blind man who says to himself that as he cannot see then things cannot be.' He looked shrewdly at Molygruber to see if he was following, and when he saw that he was he went on, 'You probably wonder where you are. Well, you are not in hell, you've just come from it. The only hell is that place you call Earth, there is no other hell, there is no hellfire and damnation, there is no everlasting torture, there are no devils with burning brands to come and singe you in various indelicate places. You go to Earth to learn, to experience things, to broaden your coarser experiences, and when you have learned that which you went down to Earth to learn then your body falls apart and you come up to astral realms. There are many different planes of existence, this is the lowest, the one nearest the Earth plane, and you are here on this lowest one because you haven't the understanding to go higher, because you haven't the capacity to believe. If you went to a higher realm now you would be blinded on the spot by the intense radiation of their much higher vibration.' He looked a bit glum as he saw Molygruber was hopelessly lost. He thought it over and then said, 'Well, you'd better have a rest for a bit, I don't want to strain your brains such as they are so you'd better have a rest and then later I will tell you some more.'

He rose to his feet and opened the door saying, 'In there with you, have a rest and I'll see you later.'

Molygruber walked into the room which seemed to be very comfortable indeed, but as he passed what might be considered a halfway mark on the floor everything ceased to be and Molygruber, although he didn't know it, was sound asleep, having his 'astral batteries' charged up as they had been seriously depleted by all the strange experiences he had undergone in hearing of things beyond his comprehension.

CHAPTER SIX

Molygruber came awake with a start of fright, 'Oh my goodness me,' he exclaimed, 'I'm late for work, I'll be fired and then I'll have to go on Unemployment Benefit.' He jumped out of bed and stood as though rooted in the floor. He gazed about him wondering at the beautiful furniture and marvelling at the view through the large window. Then slowly it all came back to him. He felt very refreshed, he had never felt better in his life—in his life? Well, where was he now? He did not believe in life after death but he had died all right, no doubt about that, so he must have been wrong and there was life after death.

A man came in wearing a cheerful smile, and he said, 'So you are one of the ones who like breakfast, eh? You like your food, do you?' Molygruber's inside began to rumble and rattle as a reminder. 'I sure do,' he replied. 'I don't know how one would get on without food, I like food, I like a lot of food, but I've never had much.' He paused and looked down at his feet and said, 'I lived on coffee and hamburgers, that was cheap. That's about all I did live on except for a hunk of bread now and again. Gee, I would like a good meal!' The man looked at him and said, 'Well, order what you want, you can have it.' Molygruber stood there full of indecision, there were so many wonderful things he had seen typed on notices outside hotels and restaurants. How was it again? He thought for a minute and then almost drooled as he called to mind a special breakfast he had read posted up outside one of the local better class places. Devilled kidneys, fried eggs, toast—oh, such a lot of things. Some of them were quite beyond his comprehension, he had never even tasted some of them, but the man looking at him suddenly smiled and said, 'Okay, I've got it, you've sent me a clear picture of what you want and there it is.' With that he laughed and turned and went out of the room.

Molybruger looked after him in some astonishment wondering why he had taken off in such a hurry. What about breakfast, where was it? The man had asked him to order breakfast and then had just walked away.

A most wonderful aroma caused Molygruber to spin around and there right behind him was a table with a beautiful white cloth on it, a serviette, silverware, beautiful crockery and flatware, and then his eyes bulged at the sight of the meal in front of him, a meal covered over with shining metal covers.

Gingerly he lifted one of the covers and nearly fainted with ecstasy at the smell coming from the plate, he had never seen food like this. But he looked about guiltily wondering if all this really was for him, then he sat down and tucked a serviette on his chest and really set to. For quite a time there was nothing but the munch, munch, as Molygruber's teeth bit into sausages, liver, kidneys, fried eggs, and a few other things too. Then there was the crackling as he devoured the toast, followed by a slurping as he drank cup after cup of tea. It was a change from coffee and he found he rather preferred it, he had never tasted tea before.

Much later he rose unsteadily from the chair and went to lie on the bed again. He had had such a meal that he could not stay awake so he lay back, let himself relax, and drifted off into dreamland. In his dreams he thought of the Earth, he thought of the hard time he had had there, he thought of his unknown father and his harridan mother, he thought of leaving home and going to work on the garbage dump and then, as he would have called it, working his way up to pushing a garbage barrow on the streets, sweeping the sidewalks. His thoughts went on and on, the pictures went round and round. Suddenly he opened his eyes to find the table had gone and all the dishes had gone as well, and there sitting opposite to him was the doctor he had seen yesterday.

'Well, my boy,' said the doctor, 'you certainly took a load aboard you, didn't you? Of course, you know, you don't need to have food on any of these worlds, on any of these planes of existence, it's just a throwback, just a useless habit carried over from the Earth where food was necessary. Here we take all our food, all our nourishment, all our energy from our surroundings. You will soon find you are doing the same because this food that you have been eating is quite an illusion, you are merely having energy done up in a different form. But now we've got to talk, you have a lot to learn. Sit back, or lie back, and listen to me.'

Molygruber reclined on his bed and listened to what the doctor had to tell him:

'Mankind is an experiment confined to one particular Universe, the Universe of which the Earth was such a small, unimportant member. Mankind was merely the temporary clothing of immortal souls which had to get experience in hardship and discipline through corporeal existence, because such hardships did not exist on what are called the spirit worlds.

'There are entities always waiting to be born to an Earth body, but things have to be carefully mapped out. First, what does the entity need to learn, then, what sort of conditions should prevail throughout the life so that the entity can obtain the greatest advantage from the life on Earth?'

The doctor looked at Molygruber and then said, 'You don't know much about this, do you?'

Molygruber looked up at him and replied, 'No, Doc, I know that people are born and that's a messy process, then they live a few years of hardship and then they die and are stuck in a hole in the ground, and that's all there is to it— well, that's what I thought until now.' He said it reflectively.

The doctor remarked, 'Well, its very difficult, you know, if you have no idea at all of what happens because it seems to me that you think a person comes somewhere or a baby is born, it lives and it dies, and that's all there is to it. But it's not like that at all. I'll tell you about it.'

And this is what the doctor told him:

'Earth is just an insignificant little place in this Universe, and this Universe is an insignificant little place compared to other universes, the universes teeming with life, life of many different kinds, life serving many different purposes. But the

83

only thing that matters to humans at present is what happens to humans. It is all something like a school. You get a baby born, then for a time it picks up and learns from its parents, it learns the rudiments of a language, it learns some semblance of manners, of culture. Then when the child is of a suitable age he goes to a kindergarten school and in that school the child is kept during school hours while the poor wretched teacher tries distractedly to keep the child fairly peaceful and quiet until the end of the school day. The first term in school doesn't matter much, the same as the first life on Earth doesn't matter much.

'The child progresses from class to class or grade to grade, each one becoming more important than the one before until in the end the school classes or grades lead up to the culmination of one's achievement, whatever it may be, what is coming next—pre-med school? Law school? Or a lowly plumber's mate? No matter what it is the person has to study and pass some examinations, and it is worth noting that some plumbers earn more than some doctors. The status symbolising on Earth is all wrong, it doesn't matter what a person's parents were, the only thing that matters in the afterlife is what THAT PERSON HAS BECOME. You can have an educated gentleman with the kindest of thoughts while he is just the son of a plumber on Earth. Again, you can have another person who might even be the curator of a museum, he might have had all the advantages of a high birth-status and he may be worse than a pig in his manners or lack of manners. Values on Earth are wrong, completely wrong, only the values of the afterlife matter.

'In the early days of this particular Round of civilisation things were rather rudimentary and crude, people learned lessons by going out and bonking somebody on the head or by getting bonked on the head instead. Sometimes the two parties would be humble yeomen or farm workers, sometimes they would be high knights jousting at a royal palace; it doesn't matter how you are killed, when you are killed—well—you are dead and then you've got to go on to another life.

'As the world itself becomes more mature in this Round of existence the stresses and strains which one may have to overcome become more sophisticated. One goes to business and gets all the hatred, the jealousies and the pettiness of office life, all the cut-throat competition in car salesmanship, insurance salesmanship, or any of the other competitive trades or professions. One is discouraged in presentday world life from knocking one's neighbour on the noggin, you have to do it by politely cutting his throat behind his back, or, in other words, getting him framed so that if, for instance, you are an author and you don't like another author then you gang up with a couple of other authors and you frame your victim. You produce a lot of false evidence and then you get a pressman on the job, you pay him a dollop of money and if he is a drinking sort of fellow you wine him and dine him, then he goes and writes an article about the victim and all the other silly creeps in the media— a most low profession or trade—lap it up hook, line and sinker, and they do their best to damn the author they have never even read or met. That is called civilisation.'

The doctor paused and said, 'I hope you're taking all this in, if not you'd better stop me, I've got to teach you something because you seem to have learnt nothing at all in your Earth life.'

Molygruber nodded, he was going a bit crosseyed by now, and so the doctor continued:

'After one has decided in the astral world what is needed, then circumstances are investigated and suitable prospective parents are selected. Then when the husband and wife on Earth have done their stuff the entity in the astral is prepared and he "dies" to the astral world and is shoved out into the mundane world as a baby. In almost every instance the trauma of getting born is so severe that he forgets all about his past life, and that is why we get people saying, "Oh, I didn't ask to be born, don't blame me for what I've done!"

'When a person dies to the Earth he or she will have reached a certain status of understanding, he or she may have learned something of metaphysics, and so will have gained knowledge which helps in the next world. In a case

85

like yours, Molygruber, you seem to be singularly bereft of all knowledge of life after death so this is what it is like.

'If a person has only lived a very few lives on the Earth plane—the three dimensional plane—then when they leave the Earth, or "die" as it is miscalled, the astral body or soul or whatever you like to call it is received into a low-grade astral world suitable for the knowledge of the person who has just arrived. You can say a human boy or man doesn't know much so he had to go to night classes, he can't climb up in society until he has learned enough to take his place in a higher society. It is quite the same in the astral worlds; there are many, many astral worlds, each one suitable for a particular type of person. Here in this world which is in the low-astral of a fourth dimension you will have to learn about metaphysics, you will have to learn how to think so that you may get clothing, food, and anything else you need. You need yet to go to the Hall of Memories where you will see all that you have done in your past life, and you will judge yourself. And I may say that no one judges one more harshly than one's Overself. The Overself can be likened to the soul. Briefly, there are about nine "dimensions" available in this particular sphere of activity. When one has finally reached embodiment in the ninth body or Overself then one is prepared to go up to higher realms and learn higher things. People, entities, are always striving to climb upwards like plants striving to reach toward the light.

'This is a low-astral world where you will have many lessons to learn. You will have to go to school and learn many facts of life on Earth, many facts of life in the astral. Then later you will decide what type of lessons you have to learn. When all that has been decided upon you will be able to return to the Earth to suitable parents and it is hoped that this time you will have more opportunities to climb upwards and to get a better status on the Earth, a better soul status, that is, not just one's class on the Earth. It is hoped that in the next life you will learn a lot so that when you leave the Earth body again you will not come to this low stage but you will move upwards perhaps two, perhaps

86

three "planes" above this one.

'The higher you climb in the astral planes the more interesting your experiences and the less suffering you can endure, but you have to approach things like that carefully, gently, and slowly. For example, if you were suddenly put upon an astral world two or three stages above this you would be blinded by the intensity of the emanations from the Guardians of that world, so the sooner you learn that which you have to learn the sooner you can go back to Earth and prepare for a higher stage.

'Let us say that a very, very good man indeed leaves the Earth, the three dimensional Earth from which you have so recently arrived. If the man is truly spiritual he could go up two or three stages, and then he would not find harsh treatment such as that which you get on this plane, he would not find that he had to imagine food to eat. His body essence would absorb all the energy it needed from the surroundings. You could do that as well but you are uneducated in such things, you cannot understand much about spirituality as witness the admitted fact that until now you have not believed in life after death. Upon this plane, this plane where you now reside, there are many, many people who did not believe there is life after death: they are here to learn that there is!

'In later incarnations you will strive up and up so that each time you die to the Earth world and are reborn to an astral world, you will climb to a higher plane and will have greater and greater time between incarnations. For instance, in your own case; suppose you were discharged from your employment on Earth. Well, in your particular job there are usually plenty of vacancies, you could get a similar job the next day, but if you were a professor or something, to give you an illustration, you would have to try harder and wait longer to get suitable employment. Similarly, on this plane on which you are now lodged you could be sent back to the Earth world in a month or two, but when one gets to higher planes one has to wait longer in order to recover from the psychic shocks endured on the Earth.'

Molygruber sat up straight and said, 'Well, it's all beyond

me, Doc, guess I'll have to set to and learn something, eh? But can one speak to people on Earth from here?'

The doctor looked at him for some moments and then said, 'If the matter is considered urgent enough, yes, under certain conditions and circumstances a person on this plane can get in touch with someone on the Earth. What have you in mind?'

Molybruger looked a bit self-conscious, he looked at his feet, he looked at his hands and he twiddled his thumbs, then he said, 'Well, the guy that's got my old barrow, I don't like the way he's treating that barrow, I looked after it, I polished it with steel wool and kept it as clean as clean could be. That fellow's got it all cabbed up with dirt. I wanted to get in touch with the superintendent at the depot and tell him to give the new man what took over my job a kick you-know-where.'

The doctor looked quite a bit shocked and said, 'But, my good man, that is a thing you have to learn, you have to learn not to indulge in violence and not to judge another person harshly. Of course it is extremely laudable that you cleaned your own work vehicle but another man may have a different method of using his time. No, certainly, you cannot get in touch with your superintendent for such a frivolous reason. I suggest you forget about your life on Earth, you are not there now, you are here, and the sooner you learn about this life and this world the sooner will you be able to make progress because you are here to learn and to learn only so that you can be sent back to—if you earn it—a higher status.'

Molygruber sat there on the bed drumming his fingers on his knees. The doctor watched him in some curiosity wondering how it was that on Earth people could live for a number of years and still be 'a soul encased in clay' hardly knowing what went on about them, knowing nothing of the past or of the future. Suddenly he said, 'Well, what is it?' Molygruber looked up with a start and replied, 'Oh, I've been thinking of things and I understand I'm dead. Now, if I'm dead, why do I seem solid? I thought I was a ghost?

Why do you seem solid? If you are a ghost you should be like a whiff of smoke.'

The doctor laughed and said, 'Oh, the number of times I've been asked that! The answer is very, very simple; when you are on Earth you are of basically the same type of material as all the others around you so you see each other as solid, but if a person—me, for example—came from the astral world and went down to the Earth I would be so tenuous to the solid Earth people that either they would not see me or they would see right through me. But here you and I are of the same material, same density of material, so to each other we are solid, all the things about you are solid. And, mark this well, when you get to higher planes of existence your vibrations will be higher and higher so that if a person from, let us say, the fifth level came to us now we should not see him; he would be invisible to us because he would be of finer material.'

Molygruber just could not take it in, he sat there looking uncomfortable, looking embarrassed and twiddling his fingers around.

The doctor said, 'You don't follow me at all, do you?'

'No,' replied Molygruber, 'not at all.'

The doctor sighed and said, 'Well, I suppose you know a little about radio, you've listened to radio sets. Now you know you cannot get FM radio on a set designed for AM only, and you cannot get AM on a radio designed for FM only. Well, that should give you a line of thought because you can say that FM is high frequency and AM is low frequency. In the same way you can say that we on this plane of existence are high frequency and the people of Earth are low frequency, and that should enable you to realise that there are more things in heaven and on Earth than you know about, but now you are here you've got a few things to learn.'

Molygruber suddenly had a flash picture of when he used to go to Sunday School—well, for two or three Sundays only, but it still came to his mind. He stopped twiddling with his fingers, he stopped fiddling with his toes, and he looked at the doctor. 'Doc,' he asked, 'is there any truth in it that people who are real holy Joes get a front seat in heaven?'

The doctor laughed outright and said, 'Oh dear, oh dear, so many people have that crazy idea. No, there is no truth at all in it. People are not judged on which religion they follow, but they are judged on the inner workings of their mind. Do they do good to try to do good or do they do good as a sort of insurance for when they die to the Earth? Well, that's a question one has to be able to answer. When people pass over, at first they see and experience what they expect to see and what they expect to experience. For instance, if an ardent Catholic has been brought up on a diet of angels, heavenly music, and a lot of saints playing harps then that is what they will see when they pass over. But when they do realise that all that is sham—hallucination—then they see the True Reality and the sooner they see it the better for them.' He stopped and looked very seriously at Molygruber before going on, 'There is one good thing to be said for people like you; they have no false ideas about what they are going to see. Many of the people of your type keep an open mind; that is, they neither believe nor disbelieve and that is a lot better than being too slavish in the following of any particular discipline.'

Molygruber sat very still, his face puckered in a frown so deep that his eyebrows almost met, and then he said, 'I was scared out of my pants when I was a younker. I was always being told that if I didn't do what I was told I would go to hell, and a lot of devils would prod me—well, YOU know where, with redhot toasting forks and I would suffer a lot of pain. How come if God is so great, if God is our kind benevolent Father, then how come that He wants to torture us for ever and a day? That's what I can't understand!'

The doctor sighed deeply, deeply, and then after some slight pause he said, 'Yes, that's one of the biggest difficulties we have, people have been given false values, they have been told false things, they have been told that you will go to hell and will suffer eternal damnation. Now, there isn't a word of truth in that; hell is the Earth. Entities go to Earth to experience, mainly through hardship, and learn, again mainly through hardship, all the various things which they have to learn. Earth is usually a place of suffering. If a person has a low state of evolution then usually he or she doesn't have enough of what we call karma to have to suffer in order to learn. They stay on Earth to gain some experience by watching others, and then later they come back for their hardships. But there is no hell after the life on Earth, that is illusion, that is false teaching.'

Molygruber said, 'Well then, how did so much about hell get in the Good Book?'

'Because,' responded the doctor, 'in the time of Christ there was a village named Hell. It was a village on the outskirts of very high land, and outside the village there was a quaking bog which was smoking hot and with a continual stench of sulphur fumes and brimstone. If a person was accused of something he was brought to the village of Hell so that he could endure the ordeal of passing through Hell—passing through the smoking bog of sulphur and brimstone —in the belief that if he was guilty the heat would overcome him and he would fall to the ground and be burned up by the heat of the bog. But if he was innocent, or if he had enough money to bribe the priests in charge of the place so that they could put a coating on his feet, then he could go all the way through the bog and emerge safely on the other side, then he would be considered as an innocent man. We get the same thing now, don't we, with the way justice is often bought and the innocent get imprisoned while the guilty go free.'

'There is another thing that puzzles me,' said Molygruber. 'I've been told that when one dies there are helpers on the Other Side, wherever that is, who come and help a person get into Heaven or the Other Place. Well, I'm supposed to have died but I sure didn't see any helpers. I had to get there all on my own just like a baby being born unexpectedly. Now, what's all this about helpers?'

The doctor looked at Molygruber and said, 'Well, of course there are helpers helping those who want to be helped, but if a person—you, for instance—will not believe in anything then you can't believe in helpers either, so if you can't believe in helpers they cannot get close to you to help you. Instead you are encased in the thick black fog of your own ignorance, your own lack of belief, your own lack of understanding. Oh yes, definitely there are helpers who come if they are permitted to come. In the same way, usually one's parents or relatives who have passed over come to greet the one newly arrived in the astral planes of existence. But this particular plane is the lowest plane, that which is the nearest to the Earth, and you are here because you did not believe in anything. So, because you were so ignorant, you find it even more difficult to believe in higher planes than this so you are here in what some people regard as Purgatory. Purgatory means to purge, a place of purging, and until you are purged of your lack of belief then you cannot progress upwards. And so because you are in this plane you cannot meet those who have been friendly with you in other lives, they are so much higher.'

Molygruber stirred uncomfortably and said, 'Gee, I sure seem to have upset the apple cart, so what happens now?' With that the doctor rose to his feet and signalled for Molygruber to do likewise. He said, 'You have to go to the Hall of Memories now where you will see every event of your life on Earth. Seeing those events you will judge what you have done successfully, you will judge what you have done unsuccessfully, and then you will have the nucleus of an idea in your mind as to what you have to do to improve yourself in a next Earth life. Come.'

With that he walked to the wall and an opening appeared. He and Molygruber passed through and moved along to the big hall again. The doctor walked to a man sitting at a desk and they had a short conversation. Then the doctor returned to Molygruber and said, 'This way, we turn down here.' Together they walked down a long corridor and out into the open to a long grassy sward, at the far end of which there was a peculiar building which looked as if it was made of crystal reflecting all the colours of the rainbow, and many other colours which Molygruber simply could not name. They stopped outside the door and the doctor said, 'There, that is the Hall of Memories, there is one on every plane of existence after one gets beyond the Earth plane. You go in there and you see before you a simulacrum of the Earth floating in space. As you walk toward it you will have a sensation of falling, falling, then it will seem as though you were upon the Earth watching all that happens, seeing all but not being seen. You will see everything that you have done, you will see actions you have taken and how they have affected other people. This is the Hall of Memories, some call it the Hall of Judgement, but of course there is no great judge sitting in solemn state who will look you up and down and then weigh your soul in the balance to see if it is wanting, and then, if it is, toss you into eternal fires. No, there is nothing like that. In the Hall of Memories each person sees himself or herself, and each person judges whether he or she has been successful. If not, why not and what can be done about it. Now,' he took Molygruber's arm and urged him gently forward, 'I leave you here. Go into the Hall of Memories, take as much time as is required, and when you come out another person will be waiting for you. Goodbye.'

With that he turned and walked away. Molygruber stayed there with a strange feeling of dread. He did not know what he was going to see, and he did not know what he was going to do about what he was going to see. But he showed no sign of moving, he seemed like a statue—a statue of a street sweeper without his barrow—and at last some strange Force turned him gently and pushed him along in the direction of the Portal of the Hall of Memories. Molygruber entered.

And so it came to pass that Leonides Manuel Molygruber entered unto the Hall of Memories, and there he saw the history of himself and his associates since the beginning of time as an entity.

He learned much, he learned of the mistakes of the past, he learned of things for which to prepare for the future, and by means unknown on the Earth his comprehension was expanded, his character purified, and Leonides Manuel Molygruber left the Hall of Memories at some undetermined time—it may have been days later, it may have been weeks later, or it may have been months later—and then he sat down with a group of counsellors and planned his return to Earth so that, a task having been completed during the next life, he could return again to a much better plane of astral life.

CHAPTER SEVEN

The great President slumped back in his luxurious swivel chair clutching grimly at his chest. There was that pain again, that awful nagging, gnawing pain which made him think that his chest was being squeezed in a vice. He sat back gasping, wondering what he should do. Should he call the doctor and go to hospital, or should he stick it out for a little longer?

Mr. Hogy MacOgwascher, the president of Glittering Gizmos, was a man in deep, deep trouble, trouble very similar to that which had terminated the life of his father. The firm, founded by his father, was prospering so much that Hogy wished that his father could be with him to witness the success. But Hogy leaned back in his chair and started groping for his amyl nitrate capsules. Breaking it in a paper handkerchief he felt the fumes going into his chest giving him relief, relief for a time. With Hogy's ailment there would be no real relief until life itself terminated the pain, but amyl nitrate kept him going for the time and he was grateful for it. He felt that his work was not finished yet, he thought of his father long dead, thought of how they used to talk together more like two brothers than father and son. He glanced at his wide picture window with the tinted glass across the top, he thought of the time when his father had stood beside him and put his arm around his shoulder. Together they had looked at the factory building and the father had said, 'Hogy, m'boy, one day all this will be yours. Look after it, look after it well, it's my brainchild, Hogy, it will keep you in comfort and prosperity for all the days of your life.' Then his father had sat down heavily in his chair and—like Hogy now—had clasped his chest with his two hands and groaned with the pain.

Hogy had really loved his father. He remembered how he had sat across from his father one day on the desk which seemed to callers to be acres in extent, highly polished, a wonderful desk indeed, hand-carved by an old craftsman in Europe. Hogy had said, 'Father, how do we get such a peculiar name? I can't understand it. Many people have asked me and I have never been able to tell them. You've got some time this afternoon, Father, the Board meeting went off well, tell me what happened before you came to Canada.'

Father MacOgwascher leaned back in his chair—the chair upon which Hogy now sat—and lit an immense Havana cigar. Then puffing comfortably he swung his feet up onto the desk, folded his hands across his ample stomach and said, 'Vell, vell m'boy, ve comes from Upper Silesia in Europe. Ve vas de Juden but your mutter and I ve vas told that even in Canada there was the discrimination against us Judes so your mutter and I ve said vell ve vill take care of that real fast, ve vill become Katholics, dey seem to have the most money and dey has the most saints to look after them. Your mutter and I, ve looked around and ve talked of different names vat ve should have, and then I thought of your uncle's cousin on your mutter's side. Good man vas he, he make good living too, he vas Jude just like you and me but he made good living vashing hogs. He gots hogs all vashed up real good and clean and proper, he scrubbed de petrol in dey hides and they comed clean just like a baby's backside, they had a rosy glow on them just like a slapped baby's backside, and de judges dey always said, vell, vell, de hog

95

him must from a certain man have comed, dey vast so good and prettified.' Hogy's father had swung his feet down to the floor again while he leisurely reached out for his special knife which had a spear point attached to it. With that he jabbed the butt end of his cigar which was not drawing any too well, then having got the smoke flowing as he wanted, he resumed his talk:

'I said to mine frau dat is vat ve vill do, ve vill call ourselves Hogswascher, dat seems to be a good name American continentwise, de has dey funny names there.' He had stopped a while and rolled his cigar about between his lips before continuing, 'Mine frau she say to me ve should do something to make prettified up more Katholic, so she say ve got have a "Mac" like dey do with the Irishers, de Irishers dey had the Mac on dey name which sort of keeps them out of storms people say mit that Irish must be. So I said to mineself and I said to mine frau at the same time dat is vat ve vill do, ve vill call mineself MacOgwascher, and from now on ve have to be the Katholics.'

Again the old man had stopped while he ruminated a bit more. Hogy always knew when his father was in a contemplative mood because the inevitable cigar was rolled backwards and forwards between his parent's lips. And then there came a great burst of smoke again and his father said, 'Mine friends I told of this and dey said to me saints in plenty you should have, special patron saint you should have like dey do with the Katholics in Ireland. So I did not know vat to have for saints, I'd never spoke nohow to no saints, so my friend he say to me, you vant a good saint? Then a good saint for you your patron saint should be St. Lucre.'

Hogy had looked at his father in amazement and said, 'Well father, I've never heard of St. Lucre. When I went to the Seminary the Brothers there used to teach us all about saints but they never taught me anything about St. Lucre.'

'Ya, ya m'boy,' said Father MacOgwascher, 'then I vill tell you vhy the saint he got that name. Mine friend he say to me, Moses, he say, you alvays vas one for running after the filthy lucre, you say to me many times, Moses, money has no smell, but others say he is running after filthy lucre so vat better saint could you have, Moses, than St. Lucre?'

But now Hogy shuddered as a fresh spasm of pain wracked his chest. For the moment he thought he was going to die, he felt that his chest was being crushed, squeezed, the air being squeezed out of his lungs, but once again he sniffed at the amyl nitrate and gradually the pain eased. Gingerly and, oh, so cautiously he moved slightly and found that the main pain had ended, but he decided it would be a good idea to stop for a bit, put work aside for a bit, have a rest, think about the past.

He thought again about his father. Years before his father had started the business on what he called a shoestring. The father and the mother had left Upper Silesia after one of the annual pogroms there and had come to Canada where they had become Landed Immigrants. Father Moses found there was no work for him so he went into farming for a time acting as a farm labourer instead of the skilled jeweller for which he had been trained. One day he saw another farm labourer playing about with a small stone which had a hole in it. The man, on being questioned, had told him that it brought much peace of mind when he played with this stone and so he kept it with him, and when the Boss farmer told him off for being too slow or too dumb he played about with this polished stone and then calmness swept over him.

Hogy's father had thought about that stone for days, and then he came to a great decision. He got together all the money he could, he borrowed money, and he worked like a slave to get more, and then he started a little business called Glittering Gizmos. They made little things which had no earthly use at all but most of them were gilded by the vacuum process and people thought when they had these golden objects in their pockets that they became tranquil. A friend once asked him, 'What IS this thing, Moses, what good does it do?'

Moses replied, 'Ah my friend, that is a good question. Vat is a glittering gizmo? No one knows, but dey vant to know so dey spends good money buying them to find out. No one knows vat it is. No earthly use has ever been found for one but ve advertise it as "NEW—NEW—NEW," and it has now become a status symbol to own one, in fact for a special charge ve vill have a person's initials engraved on it. You must remember that here on this American continent anything new is that vat dey vant, anything old it is garbage. Vell, ve takes garbage and ve gild it up a bit to make it look prettified and ve advertise it as the latest thing, guaranteed to do this and guaranteed to do that. But of course it doesn't do a thing, the buyer does the good by the way he or she is thinking, and if dey think there is nothing in it then they don't like to admit they have been conned so they tries to sell the things to show others that have been conned also. I makes for mineself quite a packet.'

'Good gracious, Moses,' exclaimed his friend, 'don't tell me that you are selling RUBBISH to the unsuspecting public?'

Moses MacOgwascher had raised his grey eyebrows in mock horror and then said, 'Goodness me, mine friend, you don't think I would be swindling the public, do you? Are you calling me a crook?'

The friend laughed at him and replied, 'Whenever I meet a Catholic who has the first name of Moses I wonder what made him change from a Jew into a Catholic.'

Old Moses had laughed heartily and told his friend the story of his life, building up a business in Upper Silesia, being famed for good quality, being famed for fair dealing and low prices, and then he said jovially, 'It all went "pffuft". The Russians came along and they took everything, they makes me a pauper and they turned me from mine house and I vas an honest man giving good deals and selling genuine articles. So I turn mineself around, I becomes a dishonest man selling junk for high prices and people respect me more! Look at me now, I have mine own business, mine own factory, mine own Cadillac, and I have mine patron saint, St. Lucre!' He laughed aloud as he went to a little cabinet fixed to one corner of his office. Slowly he unlocked the door, slowly he turned to his friend and said, 'Kommen Sie hier.'

His friend laughed with glee as he jumped to his feet

crying out, 'Moses. You're speaking the wrong language. You don't speak German now, you are supposed to be a Canadian citizen, you should say, "Get a load of this, bud".'

He walked over to where old Moses was tantalisingly holding the cupboard door barely ajar. Then suddenly the cupboard door was swung wide open and the friend saw an ebony plinth and upon the ebony plinth the dollar sign in gold stood up, and on the top of the dollar sign there was a halo. He looked at old Moses without comprehension and Moses laughed aloud at his expression. 'That is mine saint, mine St. Lucre,' he said. 'Filthy lucre is money, mine saint is clean dollars.'

But now Hogy was feeling a lot better. He pressed his intercom button and called to his secretary, 'Come in, Miss Williams, come in.' A very businesslike young woman entered and sat demurely at the edge of the desk. 'I want you to call my attorney, I want him to come here to see me, I think it is time I made my Will.'

'Oh, Mr. Hogy,' said the secretary in alarm, 'You do look pale, do you think I should get Dr. Johnson to come along to see you?'

'No, no, my dear,' said Hogy, 'I think I have been working too hard and one can't be too careful, you know. So you just call the attorney and ask him to come and see me at ten o'clock tomorrow morning here, and that is all the business we will do this afternoon.' He gestured with his hand and the secretary went out again, wondering if Hogy MacOgwascher had a premonition that he was going to die or something.

Hogy sat back in the chair thinking of the past and the future as well, as he supposed his father had sat on numerous occasions. He thought of what he had heard from Miss Williams, and then his mind drifted to the life of Father MacOgwascher; Miss Williams told Hogy about how she had gone into the office and found Father MacOgwascher sitting silent and sombre at his desk. As she came in he was looking up at the sky watching wispy clouds as they sped over his factory buildings. Then he moved and uttered a deep, deep sigh. Miss Williams stopped and looked at the old man, seriously afraid that he was going to die in front of her. 'Miss Villiams,' he had said, 'mine car I should have already. Tell the chauffeur to come to the front right now, home I should go.' Miss Williams gave her urbane, business-like acknowledgement and Father MacOgwascher sat back with his hands clasped against his ample paunch. Soon his office door opened and Miss Williams came in again looking with great concern as she saw him hunched up at his desk. 'The car is at the door, sir,' she said, 'may I assist you with your coat?'

The old man stood up somewhat shakily and said, 'Oy, oy, Miss Villiams, you think maybe too old I am getting, hey?' The secretary smiled and walked across to him carrying his coat. Clumsily he put his arms into the sleeves and she moved around to the front and carefully pulled the coat down and then buttoned it for him. 'Here is your briefcase, sir,' she said. 'I haven't seen your new Cadillac, you know, I will see you down to your car if you don't mind.' The old man grunted acquiescence and together they moved into the elevator and down to the street.

The uniformed chauffeur had jumped to attention and quickly opened the car door. 'No, no m'boy, no no, I vill sit in front with you for a change,' said the old man as he shuffled around and got into the front of the car. With a wave to Miss Williams he settled and the chauffeur drove off.

Mr. MacOgwascher Senior lived away in the country, some twenty-five miles distant from his office, and he looked about him as the car sped through traffic and out into the suburbs beyond—looked about him as though he had never seen the scenery before or as though he were seeing it for the last time. In somewhat less than an hour, for the traffic was quite heavy, the car drew up in front of MacOgwascher Mansion. Mrs. MacOgwascher was at the door waiting because Miss Williams, like a good secretary, had telephoned Mrs. MacOgwascher to say that she thought the Boss was having an attack of something.

'Ah Moses, ah Moses, I have been so worried about

you this day,' said Mrs. MacOgwascher, 'I think you have been doing too much maybe, maybe we should have a vacation. You are seeing too much of that office.'

Old Moses had dismissed the chauffeur and walked somewhat wearily into his house. It was the house of a wealthy man but of a wealthy man who had not got too much taste. There were priceless antiques and garish modern things side by side, but somehow the furnishings and the furniture, old and new, blended together in that almost mystical way which old Jews from Europe had so that instead of a hodge-podge almost like a junk shop the interior was quite attractive.

Mrs. MacOgwascher took her husband's arm and said, 'Come and sit down Moses, you look as if you could fall at any moment. I think I will send for Dr. Johnson.'

'No, no, mamma, no no. Ve have things vat ve got to talk of before Dr. Johnson ve vill call in,' said Moses. Then he relapsed into his chair and put his head in his hands thinking deeply.

'Mamma,' said Moses, 'do you remember the Old Religion? Judes is our family religion. How come I don't call in a rabbi and have a talk with him, there are a lot of things in my mind I should clear.'

The wife busied herself getting a drink for the old man, carefully putting in ice, then bringing the glass over to him. 'But how can we go back to the Jewish religion when we are such good Catholics, Moses?' she asked. The old man mused upon it as he slowly sipped his evening drink, and then he said, 'Vell, vell, mamma, when all the chips are down no more a false front should ve put up. Ve cannot return to the land of our fathers, ve can return to our old religion. I think maybe a rabbi I should see.'

Nothing more was said for quite a time, but at dinner the old man had suddenly dropped his knife and fork with a clatter and leaned back in his chair gasping.

'No, no, Moses, enough of this I have had already,' said his wife running to the telephone, 'Dr. Johnson, I call him now.'

Quickly she ran her finger down the automatic telephone

101

number indicator and then pressed a button. The latest electronic marvel whirred and buzzed as the machine churned out the home number of Dr. Johnson. After a very short interval a voice had answered and Mrs. MacOgwascher said, 'Dr. Johnson, Dr. Johnson, so quickly you should come, my husband so sick is with the chest squeezings.' The doctor, knowing that he had a very good paying patient, hesitated not one moment: 'All right, Mrs. MacOgwascher, I will be over within ten minutes,' he said. The woman put down the telephone and returned to her husband, sitting on the arm of the chair beside him.

'Mamma, mamma,' said the old man, holding his chest between his two hands, 'do you remember how ve came from the Old Country? Do you remember how ve came by the cheapest vay possible, crammed together like cattle in pens? Ve've vorked hard, mamma, you and me, ve've had a harsh life and I am not sure that ve did the right thing to become Catholics. Ve vere born Judes, Judes ve should always be. Ve should return, maybe, to the Old Religion.'

'But we cannot do that, Moses, we just cannot do it. Whatever would the neighbours say? We'd never live it down, you know. But I suggest we go away for vacation and perhaps you will feel better then. I expect Dr. Johnson can suggest a nurse to go with us to look after you.' She jumped up quickly at the sound of the bell. The maid was already on the way to the door and within seconds Dr. Johnson was ushered into the room.

'Well, well, Mr. MacOgwascher,' said the doctor jovially, 'and what is the matter? You have a pain in your chest? Ah, I expect it is another attack of angina, one of the big symptoms, you know, is a strong, strong feeling that one is going to die.'

Mrs. MacOgwascher had nodded her head gravely. 'Yes, doctor, he has had this feeling for some time, a feeling that he can't go on much longer, so I thought I should call you urgently.'

'Quite right, Mrs. MacOgwascher, quite right, that is what we are here for, you know,' said the doctor. 'But let us get him up to bed and then I will give him a thorough examination. I have with me a portable cardiograph and we will try it on him.'

Soon old Moses had been ensconced in an immense double bed with the padded quilt in the old European fashion. The doctor soon gave him an examination looking graver and graver as he did so, and then at last he said, 'Well, I am afraid you will have to stay in bed for some time, you are a very sick man, you know, you have been burning the candle at both ends and in the middle as well, and at your age you cannot afford to do that.' He closed the cardiograph machine, put away his stethoscope, and washed his hands in the luxurious adjoining bathroom. Then he shook hands with his patient and together with Mrs. Mac-Ogwascher walked down the staircase. On the ground floor he beckoned to Mrs. MacOgwascher and whispered, 'Can we go into a private room to talk about it?' She led the way into the old man's study and shut the door.

'Mrs. MacOgwascher,' the doctor said, 'I am afraid that your husband is very seriously ill; I am afraid that if there is any more exertion your husband will not last. What about your son Hogy, Mrs. MacOgwascher, isn't he at College?'

'Yes, doctor,' replied Mrs. MacOgwascher, 'he is at Bally Ole College. If you think I should then I will telephone him immediately and ask him to return. He is a good boy, a very good boy indeed.'

'Yes,' replied the doctor, 'I know he is a good boy, I have met him on quite a number of occasions, you know. But now, in my opinion, he should come back to see his father. I fear that it may be for the last time. I must impress upon you that your husband really needs nursing care day and night, and I suggest you may like to have me take care of it. I can send nurses for you.'

'Oh yes, yes, doctor, yes certainly, we can well afford it. We will have whatever you recommend.'

The doctor pursed his lips and pinched them sideways between finger and thumb. Then he looked down the sides of his nose and said, 'Well, of course, I would have liked him in my nursing home, we could have cared for him very thoroughly in my nursing home, but for the moment I rather fear that such a move might be ill-advised. We shall have to treat him here. I will send a nurse and she will stay for eight hours, and then another nurse will take over for eight hours, and I will come to see him first thing in the morning. Now, I will write a prescription and I will have the drug store send along the medicine by special messenger and you follow the instructions very carefully. Goodbye, Mrs. MacOgwascher,' and the doctor walked sedately to the door and out through the dining room to his car.

For some time Mrs. MacOgwascher had sat with her head in her hands wondering what she should do. But then she was roused from her soliloquy by the arrival of the maid: 'The Master is calling for you, madam,' she said. Quickly Mrs. MacOgwascher rushed up the stairs.

'Mamma, mamma vyfore ve don't have no rabbi come?' he asked. 'A rabbi I should have fast. I have a lot that I should talk of, and maybe arrangements could be made for mine son or an old friend to recite the Kaddish.'

'My, my, Moses!' exclaimed his wife. 'Do you really think you should have a rabbi? Don't forget that you are a professed Catholic. How will we explain to the neighbours that we have suddenly become Jews?'

'But mamma, mamma, how can I die in peace vithout knowing that I have someone to recite the Kadish for me?'

Mrs. MacOgwascher stood in deep, deep thought and then she said, 'I know, I know, I have the solution. We will call in a rabbi as a friend, and after the rabbi has gone we will call in our Catholic Father and in that way we shall be well covered with the two religions and our neighbours.'

The old man laughed and laughed until the tears came to his eyes and the pain started again. But when he recovered he said, 'Oy, oy mamma, so you think so bad have I been altogether that I need to have an insurance so one of the two can make the best bid to get me up to Heaven? Well, well, mamma, so it shall be but for mineself the rabbi I should have real fast, and then ven he has gone ve can have the Catholic Father, and in that way ve can be sure ve have covered mine passing from two sides at once.'

'I have telephoned, Hogy, Moses,' said Mrs. MacOgwascher, 'I have told him that you have had a little setback and that I thought it would be a comfort to his father if he returned for a day or two. He is coming immediately.'

Hogy sat back and thought of it all again, he relived it, for the moment his pain was forgotten thinking of those bygone days, thinking of how the big car had raced through the chilly night roaring through small hamlets and big towns. He remembered the startled expression on the face of a policeman as he jumped out of hiding somewhere and tried to flag down the speeding Hogy, and then as the car did not stop the policeman raced for his motorcycle and tried to catch up, but to no avail, Hogy had a good car and Hogy was a good driver. The policeman must have been a rookie because he soon retired from the race.

Hogy remembered reaching his father's home. Dawn was just breaking as away in the East there were the reds and blues and yellows of dawn flaring across the sky. Later that morning, after he had had a little rest so that his father would not see how tired he had been, he went to see the old man.

Father MacOgwascher was in bed wearing his yarmelke, the little skull cap which orthodox Jews wear on certain occasions. About his shoulders he had his prayer shawl. He greeted Hogy with a somewhat wan smile, and said, 'Hogy m'boy, I'm glad you've returned in time. I am a Jew and you are a good Christian Catholic. You believe in doing good turns, my boy, so I vant you do something for me; I vant you recite the Kaddish which, as you know, is the Prayer for the Dead. I vant you recite in the old, old vay which is almost forgotten. That should not interfere with your Christian Catholic belief, m'boy.'

Hogy hesitated. He had really taken to the Catholic belief, he absolutely believed the Bible and in the saints and all the rest of it. He believed that the Pope and others of the hierarchy of the Catholic Church had Divine Powers so how could he, a good Catholic, suddenly revert even temporarily to the religion of his fathers, the Jewish religion? The old man had been watching his expression, watching him closely. Then he sighed deeply and sank lower in his bed:

'All right, m'boy,' said the old man, 'I vill not trouble you further, but I believe that ve all goes the same vay Home, it doesn't matter at all if I'm a Jew and you're a Catholic, ve all go the same vay Home. If ve live a good life ve gets the good reward that's coming to us. But tell me m'boy,' he said with a faint smile, 'why do Catholics fear death more than any other religion fears it? Vyfor are Catholics so opposed to all other religions and firmly hold to the belief that unless one is a Roman Catholic no place in heaven there is for them? They must have bought all the tickets in advance, I suppose,' said the old man with a laugh.

Hogy groaned aloud as he said, 'Father, father, let me get one of the Holy Fathers here now. If you would be converted now then I am sure you would be considered for a place in Heaven. As it is, as a Jew, you have no chance at all, father, you will find yourself lodged in hell just like an old author is going to be. I have been reading some of his books lately until one of the priests caught me with them and, oh dear, I had to do a penance because I had been reading a book by that fellow Rampa. In the hospital some time ago a very good Catholic Sister wept over him and said that he would go to hell as he was a Buddhist—a Buddhist, mind, can you imagine it?'

Father MacOgwascher looked at his son with compassion, with pity, and said, 'M'boy, since you've been away and since you embraced the Catholic faith more closely you are indeed becoming bigoted. Never mind, m'boy, I vill get one of my old friends, one who has been as a son to me, and I vill have him recite the Kaddish so as not to upset your faith.'

The old rabbi came to see Father MacOgwascher and they talked together for quite some time. The old man said to the rabbi, 'My son is changed so that possibly he is no longer my son, he vould not read the Kadesh for me, he vould not even tolerate talk of our religion. I am going to ask you, mine friend, if you vill recite the Kaddish for me.'

The rabbi placed his hands on his old friend's shoulders and said, 'Of course I will, Moses, of course I will, but my own son is a very good man indeed and I think it would be

106

more meet if he did it instead, he is a young man of the same age group as that of your son. But I—well, I am one of your contemporaries, aren't I?'

Old Moses thought about it and then smiled as he nodded acceptance, saying, 'Yes, yes, that is a good suggestion, rabbi, I vill accept your advice and your son, if he vill, shall recite the Kaddish as if he vere mine own son.' The old man stopped and there was silence in the room for a few moments until he spoke again 'Rabbi,' he said, 'this author, Rampa, do you know about him? Have you read any of his books? Mine son say that many Catholics have been forbidden to read his books, what are they about?'

The rabbi laughed and replied, 'I have brought one of them for you, my friend. It tells much about death, it gives one great encouragement. I will ask you to read it, it will give you peace of mind. I have recommended it to many, many people and—yes—I know about him. He is a man who writes the truth, he is a man who has been persecuted by the press, or more accurately by the media. There was quite a little plot about it some years ago; some of the newspapers claimed that he was the son of a plumber, but to my own knowledge—to my own definite knowledge—I know that to be untrue. But I do not understand their point of view, what is there to be ashamed of in being the son of a plumber—if he had been, that is? Their Saviour, Christ, was the son of a carpenter we are told, and then many of the saints of the Catholics came from very humble beginnings. One of their saints, St. Anthony, was the son of a swineherd. Some of the saints have been robbers who have been converted. Oh no, the man tells the truth. As rabbi I get to hear a lot, I get many letters, and yes, the man is true but he got into bad odour with a group of people and has been persecuted ever since, and none of the media has ever offered him an opportunity of explaining his own side of the question.'

'But vy does he have to explain anything?' asked old Moses. 'If he has been framed, as is so often the case, vy couldn't he do anything about it at the time, vy bother now?'

The rabbi looked sad and said, 'The man was in bed with coronary thrombosis when the press people descended in quantities on his place of abode. It was thought he was going to die and the press became even more virulent as there was no one to dispute their story. But enough of that now, we have to deal with you, I will go and talk to my son.'

The days went on. Three days, four days, five days, and on the fifth day Hogy went into his father's room. His father was leaning back against the pillows, his eyes were half open, his mouth was gaping wide, his jaw sagging upon his chest. Hogy rushed to his father and then hastily went to the door and called his mother.

The funeral of Moses MacOgwascher was modest, quiet, peaceful. Eventually, after three weeks Hogy went back to College and finished his instruction so that he could take over his father's business.

CHAPTER EIGHT

Hogy MacOgwascher jerked back to awareness of the present with a start. Guiltily he looked up; how much time had he wasted? Well, time did not matter while he had this awful angina pain. He sat there holding his chest and wondering if he was going the same way as his father.

The door opened stealthily. Hogy looked up with astonishment. What was it now? Was it a robber come to steal from him? Why the stealth? The door opened a little more and cautiously, cautiously half a face appeared around the edge of the door and one eye looked at him, his secretary! Seeing that he was watching her she came into the room blushing. 'Oh Mr. Hogy,' she said, 'I was so worried about you I came in twice before and I could not get any attention from you. I was just going to phone the doctor for you. I hope you didn't think I was spying on you?'

Hogy smiled gently at her and said, 'No, no, my dear, I know you wouldn't spy and I am upset that I have caused you such concern.' He looked at her expectantly and raised his eyebrows in a good old Jewish symbol of interrogation. 'Well?' he asked, 'You want to ask me something, maybe?'

The secretary looked at him with some concern and then said, 'Mr. Hogy, during the past few days others on the staff as well as I have noticed that you have a considerable amount of pain. Can't you go and get a good medical check-up, Mr. Hogy?'

'I have had a very good check-up and I am suffering from angina pectoris, that is a heart condition, you know, and eventually I suppose I shall have to give up being President —if I live long enough, that is. And so I am going to decide who I can appoint in my place. Perhaps we should call a special Board meeting for tomorrow afternoon, will you notify the Board members?'

The secretary nodded in affirmation, and then said, 'Oh, Mr. Hogy, I do hope everything will be all right. Do you think I should call Mrs. MacOgwascher and tell her you are coming home?'

'Oh no, oh no,' said Hogy, 'My wife is worried enough about me as it is now, but I think you'd better call my chauffeur and tell him to bring the car around. Meantime I'll just wander down and stand in the lobby waiting for him, tell him to come inside as soon as he arrives.'

Leisurely Hogy glanced through some of his papers and on an impulse picked them up and bundled them into his open safe. He looked at his watch and he looked about him, then he closed and locked the safe. He looked in the drawers of his desk, then he closed them and locked each one, after which he wandered out and down the stairs.

Hogy lived in one of the new suburbs, about eighteen miles from his office. It was a long and newly developed area. Hogy looked with astonishment at all the building going

109

on; he had never taken time to look at it before, on the way to the office and on the way back from the office he had always had his head buried in important papers. But now for the very first time he looked out of the windows and saw the life going on about him, and he thought to himself, well, I suppose soon I'll be dead like my father and the world will go on without me.

'Oh Hogy, Hogy, I think I'd better call for the doctor,' exclaimed Mrs. MacOgwascher. 'I'll call him now, I think we'd better have Dr. Robbins, he knows you better than anyone else.' She bustled away and soon had the doctor's secretary on the phone. First in the well-known way of the doctor's secretary the woman was very aloof and very dictatorial with much of, 'Oh Dr. Robbins is so busy, your husband will have to come to the office.' But Mrs. MacOgwascher knew how to deal with people like that, saying, 'Oh well, miss, if you can't take a sensible message I'll get in touch with the doctor's wife, I am a personal friend of the family.'

Hogy sat down to a small meal and picked at the food listlessly. He had no heart for a good meal now, he did not feel so well, and he thought that if he had a good meal it might place a strain upon his heart. 'Well, I think I'll go to bed,' he said as he got up from his place at the table. 'I expect Dr. Robbins will be along in two or three hours, strange about these medical boys, isn't it? They seem to have no sympathy for their patients' worries nowadays, all they want is to play golf and see the cheques roll in.' So saying he turned about and walked slowly and laboriously to the staircase. In the bedroom he went through his pockets, put his loose change on the bed table beside him, and then carefully folded his clothes and donning a clean pair of pyjamas —he was expecting the doctor!—he got into bed. For a time he lay back just thinking, thinking how almost exactly his experience paralleled that of his deceased father.

'Holy Mary, Mother of God,' intoned Hogy, 'Be with us now and in the hour of our death.' Just at that moment there was the distant tinkling of a bell and hurrying footsteps. There came the sound of the opening door and low-voiced conversation, then the maid came running up the stairs. 'The doctor is coming, sir. Shall I show him up?' she asked.

'Eh? Oh! Yes, do please, show him up now.'

The doctor came in and after a short greeting pulled a stethoscope out of his pocket and carefully sounded Hogy's chest. 'Yes, Mr. MacOgwascher,' said the doctor, 'you have quite an attack again. Never mind, we'll pull you through as we have done before. Just take things easy.' He sat down on the bed and once again told Hogy that it was a big symptom of angina that the patient was sure he was going to die. 'Well,' he said, 'all people have to die in time, even the doctors. It's not a case of the doctor being able to heal himself, we all have to die, and I have seen a very great number of people die. But I am sure your time is not yet.' He paused and pursed his lips, and then went on, 'It would be better if you had a day nurse and a night nurse. I think it might reassure you and reassure your wife, who really is most concerned—needlessly, I may add—at your condition. Would you like me to arrange for nurses?'

'Ah doctor,' said Hogy, 'I think you will be the best one to arrange for the nurses. Probably you will want the same arrangement as my father had, two nurses by day and one nurse by night. Yes, I shall appreciate it if you will arrange it.'

Later a nurse came up the stairs and walked into Hogy's bedroom. He looked at her in dismay, a real frump, he thought, why couldn't I have a glamour puss for a change? Still, the nurse was efficient, she straightened up his room, turned everything about so that poor Hogy did not know if he was on his head or on his feet. Always the same trouble with women, he thought to himself, they get busy in a room and they upset everything so a poor fellow can't find a thing any more. Well, one of the penalties of being ill, I suppose, I'd better put up with it.

The night was very unpleasant. Hogy had pains and medicine and more pains, and it seemed an eternity before the first faint streaks of light came seeping in through the slats of the venetian blind. Hogy thought that probably he had never had a worse night in his life and as soon as his

wife came in he said, 'I think I'll see the Father today, I'll
have a talk with him. I think I might have a confession with
him.' His wife went downstairs and picked up the telephone
to dial the number of the Roman Catholic priest. There was a
lot of lugubrious talk from Mrs. MacOgwascher and then
he heard her say, 'Oh I am so glad, Father, I am so very
glad, I am sure my husband will be delighted that you will
be able to come and see him.'

After tea that same day the priest came. Hogy sent the
nurse out and he and the priest had a talk. 'I assure you,
Mr. MacOgwascher,' said the priest, 'that you have been an
extremely good Catholic, and when the time does come for
you to pass over you will undoubtedly go straight to Heaven,
you have done much good for the Church and I will add
my prayers to yours.' He sank to his knees in the middle of
the bedroom and said in doleful tones, 'Shall we pray together?'

Hogy signalled his asssent: he always found these things
rather embarrassing, He thought of his father, a good old
Jew, and never ashamed to admit it, and he thought that
after all he was a renegade from his own faith. He had read
somewhere that one should not change one's religion
without very, very good cause and he did not think it was a
very good cause if one changed a religion just because of
social status!

That night Hogy lay awake for a long time, just thinking.
The pain was definitely much better but still he did not feel
as well as he should, there seemed to be a peculiar hollow
feeling with his heart and at times he had the most astonishing impression that his heart was—well, he called it BEAT-
ING BACKWARDS. But he lay in bed in the darkness gazing out upon the night sky, gazing out across the trees just
close to his bedroom window. He marvelled at the ways of
life, he marvelled at the ways of religion. The teachings that
had been given to him were that unless he embraced the
teachings of Jesus Christ he had no chance whatever of
going to Heaven. He wondered what had happened to all
the souls who had lived on the Earth for the thousands of
years before Christianity, he thought of all the millions of

people on the Earth who were not Christians—what had happened to them, he wondered. Was there any truth in the teaching that unless one was a Catholic one could not go to Heaven? So thinking he sank into a deep, untroubled sleep.

For the next few days Hogy seemed to improve enormously. The doctor was highly satisfied with his condition, highly satisfied with the progress he was making. 'Well, Mr. MacOgwascher,' said Dr. Robbins, 'I'll soon have you out of that bed, soon you will be able to go away for a very, very necessary vacation. Have you decided where you're going?'

Hogy had thought quite a bit about it, but no, he couldn't quite decide. Where should he go? Actually he did not want to go anywhere, he felt tired, tired all the time. The pain was less but he could not explain why, he just did not feel 'right', there seemed to be something nagging away inside his chest. But the doctor said he was getting better, the nurses said he was getting better, and his wife said he was getting better, and when the Catholic Father came to visit him he too had said that Hogy was getting better through the grace and mercy of God.

Then came the day Hogy was allowed up and out of bed. He put on a nice warm robe and stood for a time beside the bed looking out of the window, watching the passing traffic, watching the neighbours peering—as he was doing—from behind slightly parted curtains. Then he thought, well, no good staying up here in this bedroom, I think I'll take a trip downstairs.

Slowly he moved to the door and found quite some difficulty in opening it. He held the doorknob but unaccountably he could not seem to work out how to open the door—did you turn the doorknob, did you push it or pull it? He stood there for quite a time trying to work out how to open the door, and at last by chance he turned the knob and the door opened so quickly that he nearly fell over backwards.

He moved out to the well-carpeted corridor at the head of the stairs and put his foot on the top stair, on the next stair, and on the next. Suddenly he screamed. There was a shocking, shocking, terrible pain, he turned quickly thinking that some assassin had stabbed him through the back. With that he lost his balance and fell headlong down the stairs.

The doctor, fortunately, was just coming in. He rushed to Hogy, Mrs. MacOgwascher rushed to Hogy, and the maid rushed to him. They all met in a confused huddle at the foot of the stairs with Hogy lying at their feet. Quickly the doctor bent down and knelt beside Hogy, quickly he tore open the robe and whipped out his stethoscope applying the diaphragm end to Hogy's chest.

He reached for his doctors' bag and opened it in a flash. Inside—this was a very thorough doctor—there was a hypodermic already prepared. Hogy had a confused picture of the hypodermic plunging down and there was a sudden prick of something sharp, and he knew no more.

There was a peculiar buzzing noise, a strange noise, there was a swaying and bumping. Somewhere, somewhere there was the faint murmur of voices. Hogy just could not understand what was happening. Then there was a sudden sharp blast of a car horn. Hogy opened his eyes and found that he was riding in an ambulance, he was strapped on a stretcher. Sitting on a bench beside him was his wife. She looked confoundedly uncomfortable, he thought, and then he fell to wondering why these ambulances had such uncomfortable seating for the friends or relatives of the patients.

Something else attracted his attention; what a peculiar view it was, he thought; going down a hill one's feet are higher than one's head and then going up the other side of the hill—well, it was like being on a see-saw. Things did look most peculiar. People in the streets outside looked avidly through the windows of the ambulance at traffic lights hoping to satisfy morbid curiosity. And then there seemed to be queer colours around some of the people, he did not stop to wonder why, his thoughts were just floating in and out going from one subject to another. Suddenly there was a clash and clatter in front of the ambulance and the vehicle swooped into a dark tunnel then came to quite an abrupt stop. While the ambulance was still rocking on its springs the driver and attendant jumped out and were wrestling with the door. First they helped his wife out, then with much clatter and confusion they pulled out the stretcher and did something to it which made it rise up to about four feet so it could be pushed easily. One attendant muttered to Hogy's wife, 'Go in there to that little office, you have to give every detail, insurances, age, nature of the illness, doctor, social security—everything. Then when you have done that you come up to Ward XYZ.' Quickly they grasped the two ends of the wheeled stretcher and pushed it up what appeared to be a loading ramp, in fact Hogy had a similar sort of ramp in his factory. The lighting was poor, still they knew the way, they pushed the wheeled stretcher at quite a brisk pace nodding greetings to nurses and interns as they passed.

Hogy lay back gazing humbly up, idly wondering about this and thinking about that. Then they came to an abrupt stop and he could see out of the corner of his eye one of the attendants jabbing a button, an elevator he supposed and—yes—he was right. Soon great doors opened and smartly the two ambulance men pushed the wheeled stretcher in. With a clash the doors closed and there was an 'upward movement.' It seemed to go on for quite a time but at last it stopped and the elevator rocked gently at the end of its cables. The doors opened and quite bright light assailed Hogy's eyes. With some difficulty he focused on the scene before him, the Nurses' Station just outside the elevators.

'Emergency. Heart case. Where shall I put him?' asked one of the men.

'Oh, him, wait a minute, let's see, yes here it is, Intensive Care Unit,' replied the nurse behind the desk. The ambulance men nodded and trundled the stretcher along a smooth passageway. There was muted talk, there was the clink of instruments, metal against glass, and the stretcher was turned sharply into an open doorway.

The stretcher rolled to a stop, Hogy looked about him with some confused interest. This seemed to be a queer sort of place, quite a large room and there were perhaps twelve beds in it. Hogy was quite astonished to see that some of the patients were female and some were male, and he felt hot embarrassment rise as he thought that he was going to be put to bed with some women—well, not exactly that, he thought, but in the same room as a bunch of women. He muttered something and the rear attendant bent down and said, 'Eh?'

Hogy said, 'I did not know they had wards with men and women together in them?'

The ambulance man laughed and replied, 'Oh, this is Intensive Care Unit, the men and women in here, they're too sick to bother about THAT!' But there was movement again, low voices, unintelligible mutterings, and his stretcher was pushed forward. Then an ambulance man said, 'There, you're up alongside the bed, can you slide yourself over?'

Hogy nodded his head sideways in negation, and the ambulance man said, 'Okay, we'll do it for you, we're going to slide you off the side. The two are about the same height. Here goes.'

Hogy felt himself moving and then there was a little jerk and he was more or less tipped sideways on to a hospital bed. The stretcher was removed and the two ambulance men left the Intensive Care Unit. A nurse bent down and pulled up the sides of the bed so that Hogy was just about in a cage although there was nothing across the top.

'I'm not a dangerous wild animal, you know,' he said.

'Oh, don't be upset about this,' replied the nurse, 'we always put the side rails up in case the patient falls out, it saves a law case after!' Then, as an afterthought, she said, 'Okay, hold on, the doctor will be in to see you as soon as he can.'

Hogy lay there. He did not know how much time passed, he looked up once and was dimly aware that his wife was looking down at him and then she seemed to disappear in the fog or something because all he saw was grey mist. Then he had feelings that people were about him, he felt that his pyjamas were being unbuttoned, he could feel the chill of a stethoscope and he felt a prick in his arm after which he could dimly see tubes going from his arm up to something—SOMETHING—in the distance that he could not quite see. There was a strong constriction around the other upper arm and there was the sound of someone pumping. Then a man read out some figures, after which he said, 'Umph!'

116

Then everything faded.

Time stood still. There was not any time any more. Very dimly Hogy was aware of beds being moved, or perhaps it was wheeled stretchers, there were a lot of strange clinkings going on and smells which really attacked his nostrils, he could not understand what it was.

Dimly he was aware of two people talking by his side, or was it above him? He could not decide which, but vaguely he heard things like, 'Pacemaker?' 'I don't know, perhaps we'd better keep cardiac shock probes ready, don't like the look of it myself. Still, he'll probably pull round. Let's chance it anyway.' The voices drifted off, vanishing like a vagrant breeze. Hogy dozed again and he was partly aroused from his doze by, 'Well, Mr. MacOgwascher? How are you now? Feel all right? Mr. MacOgwascher? Mr. MacOgwascher? Do you hear me? Mr. MacOgwascher, answer me, are you there, Mr. MacOgwascher? Oh dear, oh dear,' the voice continued, 'now I've got to take a blood sample and I can't get his blasted vein up!' 'Try a different tourniquet' said another voice. 'It sometimes works, try a broad band one.' There seemed to be somebody fiddling about at his side, messing about with his arm. There was an uncomfortable tightness around his upper arm, he had a feeling that his fingertips were going to burst and then there came a sharp sting and a voice exclaiming, 'I've got it, I've got it this time, it's okey-doke.'

Time passed on and the ward became more silent, there were fewer people moving about, but somewhere outside a bell was striking: One—two—three—and that was all. Three o'clock? thought Hogy. Wonder if it's afternoon or morning, I don't know, I don't know what's happening. Oh well, it can't be helped.

Voices again. 'Do you think he should have Extreme Unction, Father?' asked a soft voice. 'Well, we shall have to consider it, the signs are not good, are they? We shall have to consider it.' Hogy tried to open his eyes, it was very strange, he seemed to have a black man standing above him. He wondered if he could be in Heaven with a black saint or something, but then he realised that a hospital chaplain

117

was bending over him.

Time went on. The ward was lit dimly and from strange instruments or machines little lights flickered and went out or suddenly came on. Hogy could not see clearly, there seemed to be yellow lights and then red and then some green lights too, and now and again there would be a white light. Somewhere outside the window a bird began to sing. Soon after there came the soft susurration of sandals or tennis shoes or something, he could not decide which, and several nurses and orderlies came into the large room. There was muttered talk, and then the night staff went off. The nurses and orderlies prowled among the beds, there were whispered requests for information to the patients and the fluttering of papers as records were turned over. At last a nurse came and looked down at Hogy: 'Ah, you look a bit better this morning, Mr. MacOgwascher,' she said. Hogy wondered at that because the nurse had not seen him before, of course she hadn't, he thought, she's on the night staff. The nurse looked down at him then gave a little pat to the sheets covering him and moved on to the next patient.

The light grew brighter. Daylight came. Out to the East the red orb was gradually climbing up until from just a small elipse it rose up to a full round, red circle, and as the morning mists dissipated the sun shone bright and clear.

There was renewed bustle in the Intensive Care Unit: some of the patients were having a wash, others were having feedings, perhaps through a vein. Hogy in his turn was troubled; a nurse came along, took another sample of blood, and another nurse came and took his blood pressure. Then there came a doctor who said, 'You're doing fine, Mr. Mac-Ogwascher, you'll soon be out and on your feet again.' And then he was gone.

Several hours, or was it several days, passed and then Hogy was able to sit up in his hospital bed. Two nurses came and said, 'We're moving you out, Mr. MacOgwascher, you are going into a private room, you don't need intensive care any more. Do you have anything in the locker over there?'

'No,' replied Hogy, 'I've only got what I am actually

wearing now.'

'All right, then, we're going to push you out now, hold on.' And with that the nurses stepped on the wheel brakes to release them and carefully wheeled out Hogy's bed with its attached intravenous apparatus and he saw that as they neared the door another bed was being wheeled into the space he had occupied.

Hogy looked about him with the natural interest which comes to those who have to be in hospital or in any form of confinement. He saw it was a pleasant enough little room, a television extended from the ceiling, a bed and a window. At one side there was a closet and a washbasin. On a ledge by the closet there was the emergency call button and he noted with interest that there was a control on the bed so that he could switch on the radio and choose a programme or switch on the television and choose a programme.

The nurses moved the bed around to get it positioned exactly. Then they stamped their feet on the brake pedals and one nurse left the room while the other fiddled about for a time, then she too went out.

Hogy lay there wondering what next. He was dimly aware of some sort of public address system coming from the corridor outside. He focused his attention on it for a bit and then decided that it was a call system because doctors were continually being asked to report to this or that floor. He noted that his own doctor's name came very frequently, as he listened he heard his doctor's name mentioned again and with some astonishment heard that the doctor was being paged to go to Room So-and-So. Hogy was in Room So-and-So; he lay back and waited. About an hour later his doctor came in and said, 'Well, Mr. MacOgwascher, I hope you feel a lot better now, you look it, but you gave us quite a fright you know.' Hogy looked up rather wanly and said, 'I don't seem able to focus myself very well, doctor, I seem to be almost in a daze. I can't relate to things. For example, you were being paged to this room about an hour ago and it has taken me all this time to work out why that should be, and I decided that I must have been taken out of Intensive Care rather unexpectedly.'

'Yes, that's right,' said Dr. Robbins. 'There has been a very serious accident and we have had to get a lot of patients brought in, some of them seriously, seriously hurt indeed, and you made such progress that we thought you would rather be in here on your own instead of being with a large group of men and women in Intensive Care.'

Hogy laughed and said, 'I asked a nurse why men and women were in the same ward and she said that it was quite all right because all the people in Intensive Care were too sick to worry about THAT. How right she was, how right she was!' he said.

At the head of Hogy's bed, and fixed to the wall or rather built into the wall there were a number of strange devices. One was a blood testing device, another was oxygen supply, and there were various other things which had no meaning for Hogy but he was interested as the doctor unhooked the devices one by one and gave Hogy a thorough check. 'You'll do, Mr. MacOgwascher—you'll do,' said the doctor. 'Your wife is here, I think she would like to come in and see you, she has been very worried, you know.' The doctor went out and there was silence for quite a time, then Hogy looked up and his wife was standing beside him wringing her hands and looking the picture of misery.

'The Father is coming in to see you this afternoon, Hogy,' said his wife, 'he thinks that you may need a little spiritual consolation. He tells me that you are very afraid to die although—please God—you do not have to worry about that yet. The doctor tells me you will soon be home but that you will have to rest for a while.'

For some time they talked about the idle things and the important things which husband and wife so often have to discuss in times of stress. People do not bother about such things when conditions are good. Hogy wanted to know if she had his Will safely, if his insurance policies were to hand, and then he suggested that his chief assistant at the factory should take over and become manager.

In the afternoon the Father came along and Hogy said to him, 'Oh, Father, I am so afraid to die. It is such an uncertain thing. I just don't know what to do.' The Father, like

most parsons and clerics, uttered a lot of platitudes and as
soon as he decently could he made his escape, having se-
cured from Hogy the promise of a nice fat cheque for the
Church as soon as he was able to write.

The day wore on. The afternoon gave way to early evening, and early evening gave way to the darkening of the
night. The lights of the city outside came on and made
distorted patterns on Hogy's wall, he watched them with
fascination and wove quite a number of fantasies about the
patterns. Then he dropped off to sleep.

The telephone was ringing insistently, a harsh metallic
clatter, a terrible sound in the darkness of the night when
a woman had her husband desperately ill in a hospital. The
phone burred and shrilled. Mrs. MacOgwascher sat up with
a start in her lonely bed and reached out for the phone:
'Mrs. MacOgwascher—Mrs. Hogy MacOgwascher?' quer-
ied a voice.

'Yes, speaking, what is it?' she asked.

The voice replied in solemn tones, 'Mrs. MacOgwascher,
your husband has taken a turn for the worse, the doctor
thinks it would be advisable if you came to the hospital and
if you have any relatives there bring them with you. But
drive carefully, Mrs. MacOgwascher, drive very carefully
indeed because at such times people tend to drive too fast.
May we expect you within the hour?'

'Oh dear, oh dear,' exclaimed Mrs. MacOgwascher,
'Yes, we will be there as soon as we can.' She hung up and
slowly got out of bed. Pulling on a dressing robe she went
out from her bedroom and knocked sharply at another
door just a little down the corridor. 'Mother, mother!' she
called, 'Wake up, mother, I think Hogy is dying, we shall
have to go to the hospital. Are you awake, mother?' The
door opened and the elderly lady who was Hogy Mac-
Ogwascher's mother came out. 'Yes, yes, I will dress immediately. You do the same.'

Hogy looked up with a start. His mother and his wife
were sitting beside his bed. Was it his mother and his wife?
Hogy could not decide. Then what were all the other
people? Some of them were floating in the air smiling

121

benignly upon him. And then—Hogy's eyes widened—he saw an angel flying just outside his window. The angel was dressed all in white, in long robes, her wings were flapping away just like on a mechanical toy, Hogy thought. The angel looked at him, smiled and beckoned. Hogy felt a strong, strong pull, he wanted to follow her.

It was a truly peculiar sensation. The room was growing dark. There seemed to be purple shadows, a purple like purple velvet, and in the purple velvet he could see—well, he supposed it was specks of light, that was what it appeared to be, it appeared to be like dust motes dancing in the sunlight. He looked about; there was his wife to the right of him, there was his mother to the left of him, and what was that man in black doing? Mumbling away, he was. Oh dear yes, Hogy remembered it now, he was being given Extreme Unction by the priest. Hogy was shocked beyond belief because he found to his very considerable dismay that he could read the priest's thoughts, the priest was thinking that if he put on a good show Mrs. MacOgwascher could give a very good donation to the Church. These were rich people, the priest was thinking, they should be good for quite a substantial amount. So as soon as he had done the Extreme Unction he turned to Mrs. MacOgwascher and pronounced a blessing all the time thinking, 'That should be good for at least another hundred dollars.'

Hogy started to tremble. He felt most insecure. The bed seemed to be of a fluffy material and it did not seem able to contain him. His fingers clasped the bedclothes in desperation, he tried to stay in the bed because every instinct that he had was urging him to rise upwards, rise upwards toward the light.

'He's going—he's going—he's slipping,' Hogy heard a voice say, and then there was a strange rustling. He tried to cry out in terror but he found he could not speak, he found —well, he imagined himself to be like a kite. He looked down and saw that he had a sort of shimmering silvery cord stretching from him down to some stupid looking body on a bed. With a start of recognition he realised that he was gazing upon his dead or dying body. He could see the head of his wife, the head of the priest, the head of his mother. And then the doctor came bustling in, making quite a show. He unbuttoned Hogy's pyjama jacket and quite unnecessarily applied a stethoscope, and then gravely nodded his head. With that theatrical gesture he pulled up the sheet to cover Hogy's face. He made the sign of the cross, the priest made the sign of the cross, and the two women did likewise.

'Come with us, come with us,' the voices whispered to Hogy. 'Let yourself go free, we are looking after you. All is well, you are going to Heaven.'

'Yes, to Heaven, to Heaven,' chorused other voices. Hogy felt a slight jerk and instinctively he looked down. He saw that silvery cord collapsing, fading, dropping away. He saw with quite an amount of vertigo that he was flying high over the hospital, high over the city, and getting higher very quickly. He looked about him and with some astonishment found that he was being borne aloft by four angels, their wings were flapping and they were all gazing upon him with rapt attention. Together they sped up through the dark sky to the chant of, 'We are going to Heaven, we are going to Heaven.'

CHAPTER NINE

'Borne aloft in the arms of angels. Oh boy, oh boy!' said Hogy to himself. Then suddenly there was a tremendous pull on Hogy and he found himself torn away from the arms of the angels, down, down, down he fell turning head over feet, head over feet through the living darkness. As suddenly as it occurred it ceased and Hogy seemed to be

123

bouncing on the end of a piece of rubber or acting like a yo-yo. He was confused and quite disoriented, he seemed to be 'somewhere', but where he could not tell. He twisted about and then, as though he were peering through a hole in the ceiling or a hole in the floor, he saw a weird scene.

Hogy was looking down into a Funeral Home. He shuddered with fright as he looked and saw all those naked bodies there on peculiar tables and all having the most diabolical things done to them. Some were having blood drained out, others were having 'body orifices' stopped up to prevent leakage, and off in a little cubicle Hogy saw— HIMSELF! The body which he had left. He was on one of these strange tables and bending over him was a young woman with a cigarette drooping loosely from her lower lip. Hogy really started with astonishment when he observed that the woman was shaving the face of his dead body. As he watched a man hurried across the floor beneath and said, 'Do a good job, Beth, Mr. MacOgwascher was a very important man, we've got to have him on display by this afternoon. Get on with it, will you?' The woman just nodded her head and went on with her work. She shaved him very, very closely indeed, then she applied make-up. She brushed his hair—or what hair he had left on his head—and applied dye to various grey patches. Then she looked critically at his body and walked to the door of the cubicle and yelled, 'Hey boss, this stiff's ready. Come and okay, will ya?'

The boss hurried out of the little cubicle at the far end and rushed toward her screaming excitely, 'You mustn't say things like that, Beth, you mustn't say things like that. This is the body of Mr. Hogy MacOgwascher, a very important local man. I demand that all these bodies be treated with respect.'

'Well boss, you don't show respect to some of them,' Beth replied. 'I mind some of the stiffs you've tumbled in the sawdust and screwed down quick, they didn't get much, did they? But okay, have it your way, you're the boss. Okay, goodbye Mr. MacOgwascher,' she said as she sauntered jauntily off to another job.

Hogy turned away in amazement. When, after some undetermined time, he was compelled to look down again he found that his body had vanished and another body was being brought in. It was all wrapped up in a whole mass of cellophane, folded up like a parcel of laundry, he thought. He watched with interest as the cellophane sheeting was unwrapped and the body was exposed. It was a woman and the bossman and male assistant soon got her clothes off. Hogy, a most modest man, averted his eyes and in doing so he looked rather further than he had seen before and he saw one of the 'Display Rooms.' There he was, propped up in a very expensive casket and there were people gazing down on him. They were drinking coffee, he saw. One put his coffee cup down on the casket. Hogg looked down at himself and thought that he looked just like a film star the way he had been painted and powdered and dyed and shaved and all the rest of it. He turned away in disgust.

Time passed. How long? No one knows, it must have been two or three days anyway. Time does not matter in the life beyond this. But Hogy was stuck in a certain spot, and then suddenly he was moved again. He looked down and found that he was in a hearse being driven to a Church, he saw the casket taken into the Church and he saw the Roman Catholic Memorial Service. Then he saw the parson go up into his pulpit and give a Eulogy on Hogy MacOgwascher: 'This dearly beloved brother,' intoned the parson, 'is now in the arms of Jesus in Heaven enjoying the rewards of the virtuous.' Hogy turned away and when next he looked it was because of an insistent tugging; downwards his gaze swept to find that he was being carried into the churchyard. Then there followed more service, and he jumped as a great clod of earth came tumbling down onto the casket. But then he felt very foolish indeed as he realised that the body was down 'there' and he was up 'here', wherever there and here was. But with that, with the filling-in of the grave, Hogy felt free. He soared upwards with a force beyond his control and then there was a little 'clunk' and he found to his complete amazement that he was again resting in the arms of these angels. As soon as he was in their arms their wings started flapping and their faces started smiling, they bore him upwards—well, he did not know which way they were going, he would have said 'every whichway'—but they travelled at speed through a darkness which seemed to be living, it seemed to be a darkness made of black velvet. But then in the distance light appeared, a glorious golden light. Hogy strained his eyes in the direction from which the light came. They sped onwards and the light became brighter and bigger, leaving Hogy blinking with the intensity of it. Then as the angels emerged from what seemed to have been a long tunnel Hogy saw the Pearly Gates sparkling away in front of him, great golden gates speckled all over with immense pearls. There was a gleaming white wall extending from the Gates to the left and to the right, and through the bars of the Gates Hogy could see immense domes of cathedrals and spires of noble churches.

There was the sound of music in the air, holy music, 'Abide with me' music with a few bars of 'Onward Christian Soldiers' coming from somewhere else. But they approached the Gates with the angels still clutching him and their wings still flapping.

St. Peter, or some saint, appeared at the Gates and demanded, 'Who comes in the name of the Lord?' One of the angels answered, 'Mr. Hogy MacOgwascher, late of Earth, comes. We demand admission.' The Gates swung open and Hogy saw his first saint close up. The saint seemed to be clad in a long white robe like an old-fashioned nightgown reaching from his neck down to his ankles. He had a pair of wings stuck on behind which flapped easily, and from somewhere at his back a shining brass rod extended a few inches above his head and from the topmost point there was a shining golden Halo. The saint looked at Hogy, and Hogy looked at the saint; the latter said, 'You will have to go to the Recording Angel first to make sure that you are indeed entitled to enter. Over there, second door to the right.'

The angels took a fresh grip of Hogy—he felt that he was in the hands of delivery men!—and their wings started to flap. Slowly the angels bore him along the smooth, clean roadway. Along the sides of the roadway there were saints or heavenly inhabitants sitting on grassy banks practising harp playing, the noise was quite indescribable because they were all trying different musical pieces. But soon they reached the office of the Recording Angel. Gently the attendants upended Hogy so that he stood on his feet, gently they propelled him forward. 'In there,' said one, 'give all the necessary details, date of death and all the rest of it. We'll wait.' So in Hogy went and he saw a benevolent old saint sitting on a high stool, his wings flapping and looking over gold-rimmed spectacles peering short-sightedly at Hogy. He licked his thumb and pushed over a few pages of an immense ledger muttering to himself as he did so, then he stopped suddenly and held the page while his left hand extended upwards. 'I've got it,' he said, 'name—Hogy MacOgwascher, male, died unexpectedly. Yes, that's him, that's you, I've got your picture here.'

Hogy looked on dumbly. It seemed to be a peculiar process to be going on like this. The old fellow's wings were flapping about and they were making a noise as if the things were rusty. The Recording Angel jerked his thumb over his shoulder and said, 'Thataway, thataway, they're waiting for you outside, they'll do the right thing by you.' Hogy found himself moving, it was nothing to do with him, he was just moving, and he went out without going through a doorway. Outside, as soon as they saw him, his attendants started their wings flapping again and their faces smiling. They caught hold of Hogy and whisked him through the air. 'Now you'll have to go to Church,' said one. 'Yes, just as well get in the swing of things at the start,' said the other. And with that they swooped down and entered the massive front entrance of a Cathedral. Inside there were angels sitting all over the place, their wings flapping in tune to the music. Hogy was becoming more and more shocked, this seemed to be a travesty of things, but he stayed for the service which seemed to go on for an endless time, and all the way through the angels were flapping their wings, crossing themselves, and bowing to the altar. At last it was all over and all the angels flew up like a flock of doves or pigeons and Hogy was left in the empty Cathedral.

He looked about him and marvelled. It was impossible that this could be Heaven. He had been misled all the way along. This talk of angels was nonsense, this talk of people singing and going to services all the time—it was too absurd to be believed, and immediately it came to Hogy that the whole thing was ridiculous there was a sound like a clap of thunder and there seemed to be a rippling flash go down from the sky to the ground and it was as though a great curtain was rent and fell away. Hogy looked up astounded. There was his father coming toward him laughing and with his arms outstretched: 'Oh Hogy my boy,' said Father MacOgwascher, 'you did hold to your religion-bred hallucination for quite a time, didn't you? Never mind, I went through all the same thing except that my hallucination led me to see Moses. Well, now you've come out of that we can get together and talk about things. Come with me, my boy, come with me, you have a lot of friends and relatives here, they want to talk to you.' And Father MacOgwascher led the way out to a beautiful, beautiful park which seemed to be thronged with people.

The park was more beautiful than anything Hogy had ever seen in his life before—his life on Earth, of course. The grass was of a peculiarly pleasant shade of green and there were flowers the like of which he had never seen before, and he knew they were not flowers of Earth. The paths were wonderfully kept and there was not a speck of dust or litter to be seen. To Hogy's amazed delight there were birds singing in the trees and there were small animals about, dogs and squirrels, and some other animals which were quite unknown to Hogy. 'Father!' exclaimed Hogy, 'Do animals come here as well, then?'

Father MacOgwascher laughed, 'Hogy, my boy,' he said, 'you must not call me "Father" any more for to do so would be just the same as calling an actor in a play by the name he used in that play. After the play is over the actor can change his role and change his name. On the last life on Earth I was your father, but in some previous life you have been my father, or perhaps even my mother!'

Poor Hogy's head absolutely reeled under that, it was so

strange to him still. 'But what am I to call you, then?' he asked.

'Oh until we get things settled more—go on, call me "Father" if you want to, it may save complications,' said Father MacOgwascher.

Hogy was looking at his father, and then he said, 'But do tell me, where are we? This is obviously not Heaven because you are a Jew and Jews are not admitted to Heaven.'

Father MacOgwascher laughed uproariously. People looked in their direction and smiled, they had seen this sort of thing happen so many, many times. 'Hogy, my boy, Hogy, some of the concepts on Earth are completely wrong. I am a Jew, you say; well, I will tell you that I was a Jew while on Earth, now—well, I belong to the true religion, the only religion, and the only religion is this: If you believe in a God or in a religion then that is a good religion. It doesn't matter here if you are a Jew, a Catholic, a Protestant, a Moslem, or anything else. But the difficulty is that when one is taught all the old fables of a certain religion then when one comes over here one is so hypnotised by what one expects that that is all that one can see. On Earth there are people who go about hallucinating all the time, they think they are this, that, or something else. You may go to a hospital for the mentally afflicted on Earth and you might find a few Napoleons, a few Jesus Christs or perhaps a few who call themselves Moses. These people really do honestly believe that they are what they pretend to be. Take, for instance,' he pointed off into the distance, 'over there—well, over there at present there is a gentleman but newly arrived. While on Earth he was taught that when he went to Heaven he would have everything he wanted, dancing girls by the dozen, etc., etc. He is over there now living in a world of fantasy. There are dancing girls all over the place, and until he can see the fallacy of it all then no one can help him, he may go on for years and years dreaming of this peculiar Heaven which is peopled by dancing girls and loads and loads of food. As soon as he sees the fault—the same as you did with your angels and their wings—then he can be helped.'

'Food, father, food,' said Hogy. 'Now you have said something very sensible indeed, where do we go to get food in this place? I am hungry!'

Father MacOgwascher looked at Hogy and said, 'Hogy my boy, it should have dawned on you by now—listen—you came here and you thought you were in Heaven with angels all over the place, and more angels playing harps, and singing away and all that, but now you realise that it was mere hallucination. It is the same with our friend over yonder, he thinks he has dancing girls around him: he doesn't, it is just his uncontrolled imagination, as it was your imagination which led you to see angels. In the same way, if you want food—well, imagine it. You can control your imagination and you can have whatever food you need, you can have roast beef if you want to, you can have hot dogs if you want to, or you can have a bottle of whiskey. It's merely illusion, of course, but if you do go through with this rubbish that you want food then you'll have to follow everything through quite logically. You take in food so then later you have to get rid of certain things in the ordinary process of elimination. So you have to imagine toilet facilities, and you have to sit on such an appliance and imagine, imagine, imagine, and that's all it is. You won't make progress while you are just bound to the silly things of the world.'

'Well, I do feel hungry, that's not imagination, I feel very hungry indeed, so if I am not allowed to have food because it is illusion what am I to do to get rid of my hunger?' Hogy sounded quite petulant.

Father MacOgwascher responded mildly, 'Of course you feel hungry because you have had such a pattern all your life. At certain stated hours you used to take in food, and you've got a habit of it now. If instead of imagining dead meat going into you you think of healthy vibrations then you won't feel hungry. Think, Hogy, all around you there is vibrant energy, it's pouring into you from everywhere. As soon as you realise that this is your food, your substance, you will not feel hungry. To imagine meats and drinks is entirely a backyard manoevre which will delay your progress quite a bit.'

Hogy pondered the problem, and then he opened his mouth to protest—and found that he was not hungry any more! 'Father,' Hogy said, 'you look precisely as you looked when you were on Earth. How can that possibly be? You have been here some time. Surely you should be looking a lot older and, in any case, as you are presumably just a soul now—well, it's got me so confused I don't know what to believe or what to do.'

Father MacOgwascher smiled a smile of compassion. 'We all go through this, you know Hogy. Some of us can rationalise more quickly than others, but suppose I had appeared to you as—oh, let me say—a young woman or a young man, would you have recognised me as the person you knew on Earth? If I came to you and talked to you with a different voice and with different features and a different frame you would have thought it was just someone practising a confidence trick on you. So here I appear to you as you remembered me, I speak to you in the tone that you remembered. In the same way, your friends who are here, your relatives who are here will all appear as the familiar persons you knew on Earth, appear to you as such because you only see what you want to see. If I look at Mr. X. I know what I see; Mr. X. looks in a certain way to me, but your conception of Mr. X. may be quite different and so you will see a different Mr. X. It's as though we were standing facing each other and one of us holds up a coin; one of us will see the head, the other will see the other side; it is the same coin but we shall see different aspects of it. So it is here, so it is on Earth even. No one knows precisely how one sees another person. The thing is never discussed, it is never thought about. So here we appear to others as we did upon Earth.'

Hogy had been looking out across the park and he started with amazement at what he saw; there was a very pleasant lake and on the lake there were boats and there were people in the boats rowing, skulling. Hogy sat there on a park bench absolutely staring across at the boats. Father Mac-Ogwascher turned to him and said, 'Well, why shouldn't they have some fun, Hogy? They are not in hell, you know, they are doing what they like to do and that is a very good state to be in. Here they can think up a boat, and they can go out on the river and enjoy some of the sensations, although greatly enhanced here, that they enjoyed so much on Earth.'

For a time Hogy could not reply, he was too amazed, too dumbfounded, and then he burst out, 'But I thought we here were spirits, souls floating around. I thought we should go about singing hymns and reciting prayers, this isn't a bit what I expected of Heaven.'

'But Hogy, Hogy, you are not in Heaven, you are in a different dimension in which you can do things you couldn't do on Earth. You are here as a sort of half-way station. Some people experience considerable trauma in dying in the same way that babies born to Earth may have considerable trauma when they are born, they may have to be delivered by instruments and then they get some damage as a result. Well, it's the same with dying. Some people, particularly if they have led a bad life, have a hard time in getting over and getting free of the shackles of Earth. A mild illustration is the way in which you have been wanting food—you don't need it, you know, you just think up your food and your clothes.'

Hogy looked down at himself and then he said, 'Bodies—bodies. If we are souls why do we have these bodies, what do we need them for?'

Father MacOgwascher smiled and said, 'If you could appear on Earth now you would be a ghost, although more likely you would be quite invisible. People would walk through you and you would walk through them because of the difference in vibration. Here you see me, you can touch me, I am solid to you and you are solid to me, we've got to have some sort of vehicle in order to have our being, we've come from Earth and now we have a different body on this intermediate plane. Our bodies still have a soul, the soul goes all the way up to the Overself which is many planes above. We have a body here that we may learn things still by suffering as on Earth although of a much milder nature. But when we get up to, let us say, the ninth dimension we shall still have a body suitable to the ninth dimension. If a ninth dimension person came down here now he would be invisible to us and we would be to him because we are so different. We progress from plane to plane, and wherever we be, no matter the plane, no matter the condition, we always have a body suitable for that condition.'

Father MacOgwascher laughed before saying, 'You think you are talking to me, Hogy, but you're not, you're not, you are doing it all by telepathy. We don't use speech here except under the most unusual conditions. We use telepathy instead. But we have to go, my boy. You have to go to the Hall of Memories, and in that Hall you and you alone will see everything that you have done and thought about doing while on the Earth. You will see what you wanted to do, you will see your successes, and they will appear unimportant, and you will see your failures. You judge yourself, Hogy, you judge yourself. There is no wrathful God sitting in judgement and panting to consign you to hell or to eternal damnation. There is no such thing as hell—well, there is, hell is Earth—and there is no such thing as eternal damnation. On Earth you experience certain things and you try to do certain tasks. You may fail at those tasks but that isn't important. What IS important is how one tried to do a thing, how one led one's life, and you or your Overself will judge how you lived and died on Earth. You will decide what else has to be done to accomplish the task you set out to do and maybe have not completed. But come, we must not stay here chatting idly.' Father MacOgwascher got to his feet and Hogy rose with him, together they strolled over the green close-cut lawns stopping for a short time by the banks of the lake to admire the boats, to admire the waterfowl playing on the surface, and they then continued on their way.

Hogy laughed out loud as they rounded a bend in the path and came along toward a very pleasant tree which had a bough stretching horizontally from it, for on that horizontal bough three cats were lying full length, tails drooping over the edge of the bough, and the three cats were purring, and purring, and purring in what Hogy regarded as the warm afternoon sunlight. They stopped for a moment to look at the cats, the latter raised their heads, opened their eyes and smiled at the sight of Hogy's amazement. Then, having had their amusement, the cats put their heads back on the bark of the bough and drifted off to sleep. 'No one here would harm them, Hogy,' said Father MacOgwascher, 'here there is peace and trust in each other. This particular plane of existence is not a bad one at all.'

'Oh!' exclaimed Hogy, 'Then there are many planes of existence, are there?'

'Oh yes, there are as many as are needed,' replied Father MacOgwascher. 'People go to the stage most suitable for them. People come here to have a little rest and to decide what they are going to do, what they can do. Some people may be hurried back to Earth to take up a fresh body there, others are sent upwards to a higher plane of existence. It just doesn't matter where one is, one still has lessons to learn and conclusions to draw. But anyway, the afternoon is well advanced, we must hurry because we have to get you to the Hall of Memories on this day. Let's get a move on, shall we?'

Father MacOgwascher walked faster and it seemed that his feet were not even touching the walks. When Hogy came to think about it he couldn't feel the path under his feet either. It was all so frightfully strange, he thought. But, anyway, the best thing to do, he concluded, was to keep quiet and see what others did, they had been here so much longer.

They rounded a little curve in the path, and straight ahead of them was the great Hall of Memories, a white building which seemed as though it were made of brilliantly polished marble. Father MacOgswascher said, 'Let's sit down here for a few moments, Hogy, we don't know how long you will be in the Hall and it's nice to look at all the people around, isn't it?'

They sat down on what appeared to be a stone park bench. Hogy was fascinated that the bench took up his form, that is, instead of being hard and unyielding it gave a little and adapted to his shape. He leaned against the back and that too adopted the most comfortable shape for him.

'Look!' said Father MacOgwascher. He pointed towards the entrance of the Hall of Memories. Hogy followed his pointing finger and could scarce repress a smile. Slouching along was a big black cat looking as shamefaced and as guilty as could be. The cat looked up, saw them, and made a sharp turn and disappeared behind some bushes. Father MacOgwascher laughed: 'Do you know, Hogy, here on this plane even the animals have to go to a Hall of Memories. They don't speak in human terms, of course, but you won't either when you get there, it's all done by telepathy.' Hogy looked at his former father with open-mouthed amazement: 'Do you mean to tell me that ANIMALS go to the Hall of Memories? You must be joking surely?'

Father MacOgwascher shook his head and laughed outright. 'Hogy, Hogy, you haven't changed at all, have you? You think that humans are the top of the rung of evolution, you think that animals are inferior creatures, don't you? Well, you are wrong, you are very wrong. Humans are not the ultimate form of perfection, there are so many, many other forms, everything that IS has a consciousness, everything that IS lives, even this bench upon which we now sit is just a collection of vibrations. It senses high points on your anatomy and it yields to those high points and moulds to you to give you greater comfort. Look!' He stood up and pointed and Hogy looked at the place where he had been sitting. 'The bench is returning to its normal state, when I sit down on it.' He suited the words to the action or the action to the words, whichever way you like to put it, and sat down, and immediately the bench took up his anatomical form. 'But, as I was saying Hogy, everything has a consciousness, everything that IS is in a state of evolution. Now, cats do not become humans any more than humans become cats, they are different lines of evolution in the same way that a rose does not become a cabbage or a cabbage does not become a rose. But it has been proved even on Earth that plants have feelings; those feelings have been detected, measured and plotted by sensitive electronic equipment. Well, here on this world people come to an intermediate stage, here we are closer to the animals than we are on Earth. Don't think, Hogy, that this is Heaven, it is not, nor is the stage above, or above that, or even above that. Here is what we might term a half-way station, a place of sorting where it is decided what people will do—will they go up to a higher plane? Or will they go back to Earth? I have learnt a lot since I have been here, and I know that we are very, very close to the Earth plane, we are the difference between the ordinary AM radio and FM radio. FM is a lot better quality than is AM, it has faster vibrations, finer vibrations, and here on this world our vibrations are much, much better than those on Earth, we can perceive things more, we are in a state between the Earth-physical and the Overself-spiritual. We come here because we lose so many inhibitions. That is, on Earth I would have thought anyone was mad if they told me that a cat could talk, could have reason and all the rest of it. Here I learn that—yes, they do have reason, very brilliant reason too in some cases. But on Earth we do not understand that because the precise pattern of reason is different from that of humans.'

They sat there for some moments; they could just see the outline of the cat in the distance. He was looking about rather guiltily and then he seemed to shrug his shoulders and lay down in the bright light and went to sleep. Sunlight? Hogy looked at the sky, and then remembered that there was no sun here, everything was a miniature sun. Father MacOgwascher had obviously been following his thoughts because he remarked, 'Oh no, there is no sun here. We take our energy from our surroundings, it is radiated to us, and here we do not have to eat Earth-type food, we do not have to indulge in the Earth-type form of eliminations. If we take the radiant energy from here we always have as much as we want and no more, but of Earth-type food—well, there is always such a lot of wastage and getting rid of it is one of the big problems of humanity at the present time. So, remember Hogy, you don't need to think up a meal here. Just let yourself be and your body will take all the energy it requires and you will not get hungry unless you think of Earth-type food, and then, for a short time you will possibly have a craving for it.'

Just at that moment a man came by and Hogy started in real amazement. The man was smoking a pipe! Striding along, swinging his arms, he puffed heartily on a pipe and was belching clouds of smoke. Father MacOgwascher looked at Hogy and laughed again. 'Hogy,' he said, 'I've been telling you that some people crave for Earth-type food, some people crave to have a smoke or a drink—well, they can have it if they want to but there just isn't any point in it. It means that they have not evolved to the stage necessary for them to shuck off old Earth habits. That fellow is smoking; well, okay, he likes it, but at some time he will come to the realisation that it is just silly. He thinks of tobacco, then he thinks of a tobacco pouch, then he puts a hand in a suit of clothes which he has thought up and produces an imaginary pouch of tobacco with which he fills an imaginary pipe. Of course it is illusion, it is hallucination, it is self-hypnosis, but you get the same in mental hospitals on the Earth. You get a fellow who's got a lot of screws loose, some may even have dropped out, and the fellow being insane to a greater or lesser degree thinks he is driving a car or riding a horse. I remember once going to a big mental hospital in Ireland and there I saw a man in a most peculiar attitude and I asked him what he thought he was doing. He looked at me as if I was an idiot—not realising that HE was—and said, "Well, what do you think I'm doing? Can't you see my horse? The fool is tired, he's lying on the ground and we can't possibly ride along until the fool horse gets to his feet." The insane man then carefully got off his imaginary horse and walked off in disgust talking about all the lunatics there were in the mental home!'

Hogy squirmed. He couldn't understand what was happening to him. He felt most peculiar, it seemed that he was a piece of metal being drawn to a magnet. For some strange reason he grasped the arm of the bench. Father Mac-Ogwascher turned toward him and said, 'The time has come, Hogy, they are calling you to the Hall of Memories, you'd better go. I'll wait here until you come out, I may be able to help you, but when you come out call me Moses, not Father, I am not your father here. But now—go.'

Hogy rose to his feet and even in the process of rising to his feet he found that he had been drawn much closer to the Hall of Memories. In some confusion he turned to face the entrance and then found that he was almost running, he was going faster than he wanted to, anyway. But the great stone steps loomed ahead of him. Now, this close, he was amazed at the size of the Hall, the dimensions of the great entrance thoroughly frightened him. He felt as possibly an ant might feel going through the entrance to some palace on Earth. He ascended the steps, each one seemed to be higher than the one before. Or was it that way? Possibly he was growing smaller with each step he took. Smaller in his own estimation certainly. But he summoned up his courage a bit more and progressed upwards. Soon he reached what seemed to be a vast flat surface, he seemed to be on a plateau, a featureless plateau except that ahead of him there was a great door which seemed to reach up into the heavens. Hogy walked forward and as he approached the great door it opened and Hogy entered into the Hall of Memories. The door closed behind him.

CHAPTER TEN

The old monk painfully rose from the ground and dusted his faded robes. He looked with compassion at the hulking man climbing back over the fence separating the monastery ground from the public parkway. The man seemed to feel that the monk was looking at him. He turned around and stopped halfway across the fence and growled, 'Cyrus Bollywugger, bud, that's me, top feature writer. If you want to make something of it, get a lawyer.' The monk walked slowly to a rock and sat down with a heavy sigh.

What a strange thing it was, he thought, he, an elderly monk, just walking in the garden of his monastic home for the last fifty years and in spite of all the signs saying it was private property this coarse, crude fellow had come clambering over, and in spite of the monk's protestations had come up to him and prodded him in the chest with a thick forefinger: 'Give us the low-down, bud, what gives in this 'ere joint? You're all a lot of gays, eh? Well, you don't look too gay to me, but give us the low-down, I gotta write an article.'

The old monk had looked the man up and down with rather more contempt than he thought he should have shown, it was not good to be so contemptuous of one's fellow man, but this one surely was beyond the limit. Old Brother Arnold had been here for years, he had entered as a boy and lived here ever since trying to reconcile the words of the Bible with what he felt to be right and wrong. He had been discussing with himself—as was his wont—what it was all about. He could not take everything as the literal truth which was in the Bible; some time ago he had voiced certain doubts to the Abbot, thinking that the Abbot would help him to resolve his doubts and clear his mind but—no, the Abbot had flown into a furious rage and old Brother Arnold had penances for a whole week. Penances—washing all the dishes for the monastery.

Then, as now, after being assaulted by this crude media yokel, he had repeated one prayer to himself over and over: 'Lord, in Thy Mercy let nothing come too close nor seem too real.' It calmed him, enabled him to gaze on things in an abstract manner.

He had been wandering around thinking of his past life. There was the work in the mornings and the study in the afternoons, and so much—so much Illuminating to do. The paints nowadays were poor, plastic things, awful paints, and the vellum—well, least said about the vellum the

139

better. It might be all right for lamsphades but for the top grade Illumination for which he was noted modern supplies were useless. And then after the afternoon duties, what was there? The same day after day, week after week, month after month and year after year, the Vespers and then supper in solitary silence, and after supper Compline, the completion of the seventh canonical hour. After that the lonely cell, cold and draughty, with a hard, narrow bed and the inevitable Crucifix at the head of the bed, a cell so small that even a convict in a prison would have gone on strike under such conditions.

He had been walking around thinking of that, then this crude oaf had burst in to the private sanctuary, poking him in the chest, demanding that the old man should give him a sensational article. Gays? Good heavens no! Monks were not gays, they looked upon homosexuals with a certain amount of compassion but with a total lack of understanding. The old man had stood his ground and ordered Cyrus Bollywugger off. The man had lost his temper, he had ranted on about the power of the press saying that with his pen he could destroy the reputation of the monastery, and as the monk stood silent in his inner contemplation Cyrus Bollywugger had suddenly raised a fist the size of a ham and struck the old man heavily in the chest, knocking him down. He lay there in a daze wondering what ailed mankind nowadays, why should a hulking lout like this strike a frail old man almost at the end of his life? He could not understand it. He lay there for a time, then slowly, painfully, he climbed on shaky legs to his unsteady feet and tottered to sit on a rock and to regain his equilibrium and composure.

Yelling threats of 'Exposure' Bollywugger finally jumped off the fence and dropped to the ground on the other side, moving off with a rapid shambling gait reminiscent of an inebriated gorilla rather than a specimen of homo sapiens.

Brother Arnold sat there beside the sparkling sea, gazing out with unseeing eyes, with ears untroubled, hardly perceiving in fact the shouts and yells of merrymakers on the public beach, children screaming and quarrelling and shrill-voiced harridans cursing their men for some imagined slight. At last old Arnold jumped; a hand had descended on his shoulder, a voice said, 'What ails you my brother?' He looked up to find another Brother of equal age gazing down upon him, concern in his brown eyes.

'I have been insulted by a pressman who burst over our fence and struck me in the chest,' said Brother Arnold. 'He demanded that I tell him that we were all gays—homosexuals—in this monastery, and when I denied that with some acerbity—why—he struck me in the chest and knocked me to the ground! Since then I have felt unwell, and I had to rest awhile. But come, let us return to the house.' Stiffly he rose to his feet, and slowly the two old men who had been Brothers in the monastery for many, many years wandered up the path toward the great building that was their home.

That night after Compline when the monks were in their cells Brother Arnold felt considerable pain, he felt that his chest was being penetrated with hot spears. Feebly he used a sandal and banged upon the wall of his cell. There was a rustle and a voice came from outside his door, 'What is it, Brother? Are you ill?' Brother Arnold replied in a feeble voice, 'Yes Brother, will you ask Father Infirmarian if he can come and see me?'

There was a muttered acknowledgement and the sound of shuffling sandals upon the stone floor. It was strange, thought Brother Arnold, that no one monk could enter the cell of another monk, not even from the purest motives, none other except Father Infirmarian could enter and then only in the pursuit of his medical duties. Was there something in it? Are some monks homosexual? Possibly they may be, he thought. Certainly the authorities had enough rules and regulations to make sure that no two monks were together and they could only go about in three's. Brother Arnold lay upon his bed of pain and thought about the matter until he was roused by the opening of his cell door and a gentle voice asking, 'Brother Arnold, what ails you?' And so Brother Arnold told of the events of the afternoon, told of the blow upon his chest and of the falling. Father Infirmarian had been a fully qualified Doctor of Medicine who had given up the practice of medicine in disgust, not being able any longer to take part in the various rackets which pervaded medical 'science' of the present age. Carefully he parted Brother Arnold's clothing and examined his chest which now was black and blue and yellow, and then his trained eyes picked out—Brother Arnold had some broken ribs. Carefully he recovered the old man's chest, rose to his feet and said, 'I must go to Father Subprior and give a report on this, Brother Arnold, you have broken bones, you need X-ray and you need hospital treatment.' With that he turned and went out silently.

Soon there came more shuffling noises and very low-toned voices in the corridor outside. His door was opened and Father Infirmarian and Father Subprior entered and looked down upon him. 'Brother Arnold,' said the Subprior, 'you will have to go to hspital to be X-rayed and to have your ribs set and put in a cast. I will go and inform Father Abbot so that he may make the necessary arrangements. In the meantime Father Infirmarian will stay with you here in case he can do anything for you.' The Subprior turned to leave the cell but Brother Arnold cried, 'No, Father Subprior, no Father Subprior, I do not want to go to hospital, I have heard so much of the malpractice there and I would rather be treated by Father Infirmarian, and if I am beyond his capacity then I will commend my soul to God.'

'No, that will not do Brother Arnold, I cannot accept that. Only Father Abbot can make a dispensation on this case, I will go to see him,' said the Subprior as he left the cell.

There was little Father Infirmarian could do to help the aged Brother, but he moistened a cloth and wiped the old man's brow to try to reduce the fever somewhat. Again he undid Brother Arnold's vestments so that not even that weight should cause further difficulty. Together they sat for the old man was half sitting in his bed now, it being easier for him to breathe in that posture.

Soon there came footsteps again. The cell door opened and in came Father Abbot. The Subprior had to wait outside for the cells were so small that they could not take more than two people when one was on a bed. Father Abbot came and looked down at Brother Arnold and his face showed horror and shock at the state of the old man's chest. There was a low-voiced discussion between Father Abbot and Father Infirmarian, and then the Abbot turned to Brother Arnold saying, 'I cannot accept the responsibility, Brother Arnold, of keeping you here in this condition. You will have to go to hospital.' He stopped for a moment and pursed his lower lip between finger and thumb in deep thought. After some moments he looked at Brother Arnold again and said, 'In view of your condition, in view of your age, I will if you wish, Brother Arnold, telephone for the Bishop and then we can only accept his ruling.'

'I will appreciate that, Father Abbot,' said Brother Arnold. 'I am very loathe to leave this, my home, for the unknown perils of hospitals as they are of this day. I have heard so much against them that I have no confidence, and without confidence I should not benefit from their treatment. My whole faith is with Father Infirmarian.'

'As you will, Brother Arnold,' said Father Abbot, 'I should not say this in your hearing but I cannot help agreeing with you.'

The Abbot left the cell and he and the Subprior went away toward the Abbot's office where minutes after he could be heard telephoning the Bishop of the Diocese in which the monastery was located. There were frequent, 'as you say, Father Bishop, as you say. Yes, I will do that, goodbye,' and there was the sound of the telephone being replaced on its cradle.

Father Abbot sat in silence for a while and then, upon a sudden decision, he sent for a Scribe who came to take dictation and to prepare a paper which Brother Arnold would have to sign saying that if he refused to leave the monastery for a hospital he did so upon his own responsibility, and the monastery could not be held responsible for whatever occurred as a result of that decision.

The monastery gleamed cold and white in the brilliant light of the full moon. Light scurrying clouds hurrying across the face of the moon somehow lent a sinister air to the monastic building. Moonlight reflecting brightly from the many windows glittered and seemed to wink at the clouds as they scudded by. Somewhere, a night owl called loudly in the darkness, nearby there was the gentle hiss of waves lapping the sand, reaching up higher and withdrawing to form the next wave. In the monastery itself all was quiet, hushed as though even the building knew that death was at hand, as if it were waiting for the beating of the wings of the Angel of Death. Occasionally there came all those strange sounds which occur in an old, old building which is feeling the weight of the years. Every so often there came the scurrying pit-a-pat of little mouse feet running across the polished floors, and sometimes a frightened squeak from a mouse. But the building was still and as silent as an old building can ever be. Then from the clock tower the hours rang out across the listening countryside. From the distance there came the roar of a train speeding along on its iron rails toward the metropolis.

Brother Arnold lay upon his bed of pain. By the light of the flickering candle he could see Father Infirmarian gazing upon him with compassion. Suddenly, so suddenly as to make Brother Arnold jump, Father Infirmarian spoke: 'Brother Arnold, we have been so concerned about you, about your future. Sometimes you have beliefs which are so different from those of the orthodox religion. You seem to think it doesn't matter what you believe so long as you believe. Brother Arnold, at this late stage repent, repent, lent your shriving take place. Shall I call the Father Confessor for you, Brother Arnold?'

Brother Arnold looked about him and said, 'Father Infirmarian, I am satisfied with my way of life, I go to what I believe will be Heaven, I go according to my own belief, not necessarily a belief according to the book. I believe that our prescribed religion, the orthodox religion, is narrow in its concepts.' He gasped as pain wracked his body, he felt as though his chest was on fire, he felt as though nails were being driven through his chest, and he thought of the nails driven through the hands and the feet of Christ, he thought of the pain of the thrust in the body caused by the guard

144

below the Crucifix.

'Father Infirmarian, Father Infirmarian,' he called, 'will you pass me the Crucifix that I may kiss the Five Wounds?'

Slowly Father Infirmarian rose to his feet and moved to the head of Brother Arnold's bed. Reaching up, after crossing himself, he touched the Crucifix, lifted it down, and pressed it to Brother Arnold's lips.

'Father Infirmarian, Father Infirmarian,' cried Arnold in anguish and amazement, 'who are all these people who have gathered about me? Ah, I see, here is my mother, she is come to bid me welcome to the Greater Reality, the Greater Life. My mother is here, my father is here, many friends of mine are here too.' Very quickly Father Infirmarian rose to his feet, moved to the door and rapped suddenly and sharply on the door of the next cell. There was a startled exclamation from within and almost on the instant a shaven-headed monk appeared around the opening door.

'Quick, quick!' said Father Infirmarian, 'Call Father Abbot. Brother Arnold is about to leave us.'

The monk stopped not to don a robe nor to put on his sandals, he sped down the corridor and leapt down the stairs. Soon he returned following Father Abbot who had been waiting alone in his study.

Brother Arnold looked about him wildly, and exclaimed in anguish, 'Why is it that we who preach religion are afraid to die? Why is it, Father Abbot, why is it that we are so afraid to die?' An answer appeared in Brother Arnold's brain: 'You will learn that, Arnold, when you come to us on the Other Side of life. You will be coming shortly.'

The Father Abbot knelt beside the bed holding the Crucifix in his upraised hands. He prayed. He prayed for mercy upon the soul of Brother Arnold who had so often departed from the prescribed script of religion. Beside the bed the guttering candle flared and went low, a vagrant breeze caught the flame and turned it into black carbon. It flared again and in the light of that lone candle they saw Brother Arnold raise up crying, 'Nunc Dimitis, Nunc Dimitis, Lord now lettest Thou Thy servant depart in peace according to Thy word.' With that he groaned and fell back lifeless against

145

the pillows.

Father Infirmarian crossed himself and said a prayer for the Passing of the Dead. Then reaching over the head of the Father Abbot who was still upon his knees Father Infirmarian closed the eyes of Brother Arnold and put little pads upon them to keep them closed. He put a band beneath the lower jaw and held the gaping mouth shut. Then he tied the band on the top of Brother Arnold's tonsured head. Carefully he raised the dead monk's head and shoulders and removed the pillows. He took Brother Arnold's hands and crossed them upon his breast. Lower he attended to the necessary toilet, and then the sheet was pulled up over Brother Arnold's dead face.

Slowly Father Abbot rose to his feet and went out of the lonely cell, went to his own office and instructed a monk. Minutes later there came the tolling of the bell to signal the passing from life to death. Silently the monks rose from their beds and donned their robes and filed down to the Chapel to recite the Service for the Dead. Later when the sun was rising above the horizon there would be a mass, a mass which all would attend, and then the body of Brother Arnold wrapped in his robe and with his cowl covering his face, with his hands about the Crucifix on his chest, would be carried in solemn procession from the monastery down the garden path and into the little consecrated patch which held so many of the bodies of the monks from times long gone.

Even now two monks were preparing to go out to the consecrated patch and dig the grave, the grave facing the sea, in which Brother Arnold's body would rest until its final dissolution. The two monks went out with spades upon their shoulders, silent, each thinking, wondering maybe what was beyond this life? Holy Writ taught us much but could Holy Writ be depended upon exactly, precisely? Brother Arnold had always said—to the anger of Father Abbot—that one could not take Holy Writ too seriously but only as a pointer of the Way, only as a guide, as a signpost. Brother Arnold had often said that the life hereafter was merely a continuation of the life on Earth. Brother Arnold had been sitting silent and still some time ago in the Refectory. Before him was an unopened bottle of aerated water. Suddenly he had risen to his feet, grasped the bottle in his hands and said, 'Look, my brothers, this bottle resembles the human body, in it we have a soul. As I take off the cap of this bottle there is bubbling, there is turmoil in the water in the bottle and the gases like unto the soul of a human burst forth. That is how, my brothers,' he had said, 'we leave our bodies at the termination of this life. Our bodies are but clothing to the immortal soul, and when the clothing is old and tattered and no longer able to hold together then the soul relinquishes the body and goes elsewhere, and for what happens elsewhere? Well, my brothers, each of us and every one of us will discover that in his turn.' Brother Arnold had tipped the contents of the bottle into a glass and drank it swiftly saying, 'Now the body which was the water has disappeared just as the body which is our body will eventually disappear into the earth and there be resolved at last into its component parts.'

The two monks thought of that as they walked down the path and looked around for a suitable patch in which to dig the grave. Six feet deep by six feet long by three feet wide. Without a word they set to work, carefully removing the turf and putting it aside so that later it might be used to cover a new grave.

In the monastery the body of Brother Arnold was being moved, being moved before rigor mortis supervened because that would have made bending the body around the curves of stairs difficult. Four monks had a canvas sheet with handles at each corner. Carefully they slid it under the body of Brother Arnold and positioned his body exactly in the middle of the canvas sheet. Carefully they drew the sides of the sheet up so that the handles at the top and the bottom could interlock, the head end interlock together and the foot end interlock together. Carefully the monks lifted the body off the bed, carefully they manoevred it out through the doorway of the cell, and with a little struggle they managed to get it turned in the corridor. Moving slowly and reciting the set phrases of the Ritual for the Dead they carried the body down the stairs and into the Chapel annexe. Reverently they placed the body on the bier, arranging the robes to fall naturally and placing sandals upon the dead monk's feet. Carefully they replaced the Crucifix between the dead hands, carefully they drew down the cowl to cover the features. Then the four monks began their solitary vigil guarding the body of their dead Brother until there would come the light of day when again masses would be sung.

And so Brother Arnold left his body. He felt that he was being borne upwards. Looking down with some trepidation he found a silvery blue cord stretching from his present body to the pallid ghastly corpse resting on the bed below. About him he could half-distinguish faces. Surely that was his mother? And there was his father. They had come from beyond the Shades to help him, to guide him on his journey.

The way ahead was dark. It seemed to be a long, endless tunnel, a tunnel or maybe a tube. It seemed to be something like the tube which the monks carried in procession through the village on certain occasions, a tube supported by a pole which they raised up against windows so that people could give their contributions to the mouth of the tube and it would slide down to a collecting bag below.

Brother Arnold felt himself moving slowly up this tube. It was a most peculiar feeling. He turned his head down and saw that the silver cord was thinning and even as he looked the cord parted and was no more, it seemed like a ribbon of elastic which, cut, withdrew under its own elasticity.

Above him as he peered upwards there seemed to be a bright light. He was reminded of when he had gone down the monastery well to help clear the water filters below. Looking up he had seen the bright circle of light which illuminated the top of the well. He had a similar feeling now, the feeling was that he was being borne upwards, upwards to the light, and he wondered—what now?

Suddenly, like a stage devil appearing through a trap, Arnold appeared—where?—he appeared on this other world, or in another plane of existence. He did not know what it was for the moment. The light was so intense that he had to cover his eyes, and after a few moments he cautiously lifted his hands away from his eyes and uttered a weak, 'Oh, oh my!' at the sight before him. There came an amused chuckle by his side, and he turned and gazed at the one who used to be his father. 'Well, Arnold,' said the other, 'you certainly seem astonished, I should have thought you would have remembered it all although I must say—' he gave a rueful smile, 'that it took me long enough.'

Arnold gazed around. 'Well, I certainly AM astonished,' he said. 'This place appears to be like Earth, oh a much better version of it, I grant you, but it does appear to be an Earth-type world, and I thought we would be going to—well, I don't quite know what, but to a more abstract type of world, not this.' He gestured at the buildings and the parklands. 'This does look like a frightfully posh version of the Earth!'

'Arnold, you have quite a lot to learn, or to re-learn,' said his former father. 'Your own studies, your own long experience should have led you to the conviction that if an entity, a human soul, went direct from the Earth world up to high celestial spheres then it would be entirely to destroy that entity's sanity, the change would be so great.' He looked hard at Arnold and said, 'Think of a glass, an ordinary glass tumbler if you like; you cannot place a cold glass straight into very hot water, it would fracture, and there are many things of a like nature, it must be done gently, gently. In the same way with a person who has been ill for a long time and confined to bed—you don't expect him to get out of bed one day and to walk around and run around as if he were a well-trained athlete. It is the same here. You were upon a crude, crude world, the Earth, you were on the upward climb and here is an intermediate stage, let us say a halt where one can pause awhile and get one's bearings.'

Arnold looked around marvelling at the beauty of the buildings, marvelling at the green of the greenery and the trees without blemish. Here, he saw, animals and birds were in no way afraid of the humans. This seemed to be a world of good rapport.

'Soon, I have no doubt, you will be going up to higher planes, but before that can be decided you have to go to the

149

Hall of Memories. When there you may recover your flagging memory of your visit here before.'

'I am quite amused at the way we say, "up"', said Arnold, 'I thought the Heavenly Spheres and the Earth Spheres or planes of existence—call them what you will—were intermingled and perhaps even occupied the same space, so why say "up"?'

Another man broke in. He had been watching but saying naught. Now he remarked mildly, 'Well, it is up, there's no doubt about it. We go up to a higher vibration. If we were going to go to a lower vibration then we should be going down, and, in fact, there are such places of lower vibration and people here who have to go down there for some reason, perhaps to help some weary soul, would soon say that he or she was going down to plane So-and-So. But this is an intermediate stage, we come up to it from the Earth. We want to get away from the Earth and if we were going down then you could say we were getting nearer to the Earth's core, and that's what you do not want to do. So up it is, up to a higher vibration, up to get away from the centre of the Earth, and soon you, Arnold, will be going up again. Of that I have no doubt for this is just an intermediate stage, people from here go up to a higher plane or they go down to the Earth again, to learn more lessons. But now it's time you went to the Hall of Memories, everyone must go there first. Come this way.'

Together they walked along, walked along what seemed to be a very well-kept street. There were no cars, no mechanically propelled vehicles of any kind. People walked and the animals walked as well, often alongside the humans. Soon Arnold and his new friend turned away from the streets and entered a little lane at the end of which Arnold could see much greenery. He walked along with the other, both concerned about their own thoughts. Soon they came to the end of the little lane and there was a beautiful, beautiful park ahead of them with wonderful plants, wonderful flowers of a type which Arnold had never seen before. And there in the centre of the park was the great domed structure which the people termed the Hall of Memories. They stood awhile taking in the picture, the greenery, the vivid colours of the flowers, and the very brilliant blue of the skies which were reflected brightly on the surface of the placid lake near the Hall of Memories.

As of one accord Arnold and his new friend stepped upon the path leading to the Hall. They walked along wondering perhaps about the other people who were sitting on benches or lying on the grass. Frequently they would see a person mount the steps to the Hall of Memories, and they would see others coming out from some hidden exit. Some were looking elated, some were looking chastened beyond expression. Arnold looked and gave an anticipatory shudder at the strangeness of it all. What happened in the Hall of Memories, what would happen to him? Would he pass muster and go on up to a higher vibration, to a more abstract form of life? Or would he be sent down to Earth to start another life all over again?

'Look, look,' murmured Arnold's new friend. He nudged Arnold and pointed in a certain direction. His voice sank to a whisper as he said, 'These are entities from a much higher plane of existence, they have come to observe the people, look at them.'

Arnold looked and he saw two bright golden spheres, they seemed to be made of light, they were so brilliant that Arnold could not even guess at the true shape. The golden spheres were drifting along like golden bubbles in a light breeze. They drifted along and came to the walls of the Hall of Memories. They touched and went straight through without leaving a mark on the structure.

'I must leave you now,' said Arnold's friend. 'But keep cheerful, keep your pecker up, YOU have nothing to worry about, that's for sure. Goodbye. There will be someone here to meet you when you come out. Cheer up, don't look so mournful!' With that he turned abruptly and retraced his steps.

Arnold, with mounting apprehension—no!—with complete fright, plodded on to the end of the path to where the entrance to the Hall of Memories began. At the foot of the great stone steps he stopped and tried to look around to see

151

what was happening, but no, he did not stop after all, some force was propelling him, drawing him. He hurried up the steps and stopped a moment before the great entrance door. Suddenly, silently, it opened and Arnold was pushed inside, pushed or dragged inside, it does not matter which, he was inside and the door shut behind him.

CHAPTER ELEVEN

Silence, perfect silence, not a whisper of sound, not a rustle, nothing. Silence so great that there was an absolute absence of anything except silence.

Darkness, so dark that Arnold could almost see things in the light. His eyes had been used to light, they must have stored up light patterns because now in the darkness so profound he was getting optic nerve flashes.

An absolute absence of everything. Arnold moved and could not tell that he had moved, everything was emptiness, emptier, he thought, than space itself. But then suddenly a faint point of light appeared 'somewhere', and from it blue rays were flung out like sparks on a red hot horse shoe being beaten by a blacksmith. The light was blue, pale blue in the centre deepening to a purple blue further out. The light expanded, it was still blue, and then Arnold saw the world, the Earth which he had so recently left. It seemed to be floating in space. There was nothing but a mass of clouds, it seemed almost like a ball of cotton wool of different colours, black clouds and white clouds, and he had a momentary glimpse of what he thought must be the Sahara Desert, nothing but sand and desolation. Then through the Earth he saw other globes, all inter-mingling and yet not one of them touching. 'I'm going mad,' thought Arnold, 'let's get out of here!' And he turned to make his escape. Behind him he saw two glowing orbs. He stared back at them and then had an impression: 'It is all right, Arnold, we know all about you, we have been examining your past. You have done very well in this last life other than that you have been so lazy that you did not rise above the deacon stage, you did not bother to get ordained. That was lazy of you, Arnold.'

Arnold stared, and the impression came to him: 'No, you cannot see us, we are of a different vibration. All you can see is a globe of light and that is not at all what we look like. Soon you will be one of us—if you wish—and if you do not so desire then you will have to go back to Earth and clear up a few ends that you left untied such as the business of staying as a deacon when you could have risen so much higher.'

'But what are you like?' asked Arnold.

'Not everyone knows how a king lives,' thought one of the spheres. 'People have the most weird ideas about kings and queens, some thinking that they live all day sitting on a golden throne with a crown on their head and holding the Orb and the Sceptre. Kings and queens do not live that way at all. Similarly on Earth people have many weird ideas about the immediate life after death, they think there is Heaven with Pearly Gates—well, there is Heaven with Pearly Gates for those who think there is, because here in a land which is controlled by thought people are what they think they are, and if a person thinks there are angels flying about then they will see angels flying about. But it's all a waste, there is no use at all in such a life, and these inter-mediate stages are so that people can rationalise things and become straightened out.'

There seemed to be some conversation going on between the two globes because there was much bobbing and vibrating between the two. Then from one of the globes there came this thought; 'We are much amused that people on this plane of existence are so tied up with their habits

153

and customs that they even have to imagine food which they then imagine that they eat. We have seen,' the telepathic voice continued, 'some very religious people here who even have to eat fish on Fridays!'

'Holy mackerel!' said Arnold, 'that does seem a bit far-fetched, doesn't it?'

'But why do people fear death so much?' asked Arnold. 'Although I was a religious and obeyed all the rules of the Order I confess that I was terrified of dying. I thought God would be there ready to smite me down for all the wrongs I had done, and I have always wondered why people feared death so much.'

The telepathic voice came again: 'People fear death because we do not want them to know the truth. Death is pleasant, when one comes to the last stages of dying all fear is removed, all pain, all suffering is removed. But people have to fear death otherwise they would commit suicide and there would be mass suicides; if people knew how pleasant death is and how much better the life here is then they would commit suicide and that would be a very bad thing indeed. They go to Earth as children go to school to learn, and children must be kept in school and not allowed to escape into the joys of the countryside. So it is that people fear death until the last moment, until it is clear that they cannot possibly live longer. Then they embrace the warmth of death, the happiness of death.'

'But we want you to leave the material worlds and come to the worlds of the spirit,' thought one of the globes.

'But why is there a material heaven—even though an imitation one—if people do not need material things?' asked Arnold.

'Because for an Overself or Soul or whatever you like to call it it is necessary to get material experience, and in the hardships of the Earth one can learn hard lessons in just a few years whereas if the lessons had to be absorbed by a spirit living in a spirit world then it would take eons of time. But now we have to show you your past life. Watch!'

The world in front of Arnold seemed to expand, it expanded so rapidly that he thought he was falling over the edge of a precipice—a precipice in space?—on to the turning world. He fell, or thought that he fell, for thousands of miles and then he found himself living just a few feet above the Earth. In front of him there were strange looking men engaged in mortal combat, wielding spears, axes, and even sticks with heavy stones at the end. Arnold looked at them, and one figure in particular attracted him. The figure suddenly rose up from lying on the ground and put his spear right through the chest of an approaching enemy. The enemy toppled to the ground in a welter of blood. 'That was a bad deed you did, Arnold,' said a voice in his head, 'you had to live many lives to atone for that.'

The pictures went on from the times of the Assyrians on through different periods of Earth history, and then at last he saw the life he had just left, he saw his early days and the little offences he had committed such as robbing an old neighbour's orchard or taking some coins out of a milk bottle which had been left for collection by the milkman. He saw how he had gone to the market a few times and swiped fruit, apples, pears and bananas.

Later he saw himself as a monk overcome with the fear that he would not be able to pass the examinations for Ordination and so adopting a supercilious attitude to cover up the fear of his own incompetency.

He saw again his dying and his death, and then he seemed to be rocketing out of the Earth, going up and up and up, and then landing upon another plane of existence.

'You performed very well in that life,' said the voice in his head, 'and it would be a mere waste of time for you to go back to the Earth phase again. We think instead you should come to the world beyond material things where you can undoubtedly learn much.'

'But what about my friends here?' asked Arnold, 'My father and my mother and the many people I knew before, isn't it rather bad to come and take their hospitality and then suddenly go off to a higher plane? Whatever will they think of me?'

The voice in his head had a definite laugh as it replied, 'If they were worthy of going higher, Arnold, they would

155

have gone higher, and if you do not come out of this building in a form which they can recognise then they will appreciate that you have gone higher, to a higher plane of existence. When we come out of here the three of us will appear as globes of light to them, and having seen two enter and three come out they will know that the third was you and they will rejoice accordingly at your advancement and your elevation. It will also give them much hope that eventually they may do the same.'

And so it came about that in his mind Arnold thought, 'Yes,' and then to his profound astonishment he found that he felt absolutely vital, more full of life than he had ever felt before, he felt full of energy and looking down he could not see his feet any more, he could not see his hands. While he stared in a somewhat bemused manner the voice came to him again: 'Arnold, Arnold, you are as us now, if you look at us you will see how you are, we are just masses of pure energy taking in extra energy from our surroundings. We can go anywhere and we can do anything entirely by thought, and Arnold, we do not eat food as you know it any more!'

There was a peculiar singing sensation and Arnold found that he was following his two new friends through the wall of the Hall of Memories. He smiled slightly as he saw some of his friends outside, he saw the expression on their faces as they noted that three globes went off but only two had entered.

And the singing noise increased, and there was a sensation of rushing, of speed, and Arnold thought, 'I wonder why we always seem to go upwards and never down?' As he thought that he got the answer: 'Well, of course we go upwards, we go up to a higher vibration. You've never heard of going down to a higher vibration, have you? We go up in the same way on Earth when you want to change your state you get away from the Earth, you go up which is the way; if you went down you would get closer to the centre of the Earth, the thing you were trying to avoid, but—pay attention where we are going.'

Just at that moment Arnold experienced a shock or a

jolt. He could not explain exactly the type of sensation but probably if he had thought about it he would have likened it unto a jet plane breaking through the sound barrier. It was definitely a 'peculiar' sensation as if he was entering another dimension, and that is precisely what he was doing.

There was this sudden jolt and everything seemed to flare around him, he saw coruscating, scintillating colours of hues which he had never before experienced, and then he looked at the two entities with him and exclaimed, 'Oh! You are humans just like me!'

The other laughed and said, 'But of course we are humans the same shape as you, what should we be? The great Plan of the Universe makes it necessary that people shall adopt a certain shape, for example we are humans no matter if it is sub-human, ordinary human or super-human, we all have the same number of heads, arms, and legs, and the same basic method of speech, etc. You will find that in this particular Universe everything is built on the carbon mole-cule form so no matter where you go in this Universe humans or humanoids are basically the same as you or us. In the same way, the animal world is basically the same, a horse has a head and four limbs—just as we have—and if you look at a cat—well, there is the same again, a head, four limbs and a tail. Years ago humans had tails, fortunately they have done without them. So remember wherever you go in this Universe, no matter in what plane of existence, everyone is of basically the same form, what we call the human form.'

'But, good gracious me, I saw you as a ball of light!' said Arnold in some confusion. 'And now I see you as super, super-human forms although you still have a lot of light around you.'

The others laughed and replied, 'You'll soon get used to it. You're going to be here in this plane for quite a long time, there is a lot to be done, a lot to be planned.' They drifted on for some time. Arnold was beginning to see things he had never seen before. The others were watching him and one said, 'I expect your sight is getting used to seeing things here, you are in the fifth dimension now, you know, away from the world or plane of material things. Here you won't need to dream up food or drink or things of that nature. Here you exist as pure spirit.'

'But if we are pure spirit,' said Arnold, 'how is it that I see you as human shapes?'

'But it doesn't matter what we are, Arnold, we still have to have a shape. If we were round balls of flame we would have a shape, and now, here, you are getting your fifth dimensional sight in focus and so you see us as we are, human in shape. You see, also, plants, flowers, dwellings around you; to the people of the plane from which you have just come they would be nothing, not that they could come here—if they came here they would be burned by the very high radiations here.'

They drifted on over such beautiful country that Arnold was entranced. He thought how difficult it would be if he ever had to return to the Earth and describe what conditions here were like. On the Earth, or on the fourth dimensional plane there were no words at all to describe life in this fifth dimension.

'Oh, what are those people doing?' asked Arnold as he pointed to a group inside a very pleasant garden. They seemed to be sitting in a circle, and they seemed—although the idea was quite absurd to Arnold—that they were making things by thought. One of his companions turned leisurely and said, 'Oh them? Well, they are just preparing things which will later be sent forth as an inspiration to certain people on the Earth. You see, there are many things originating here which we put into the dull minds of humans to try to raise their spiritual level. Unfortunately the people of the Earth want to use everything for destruction, for war, or for capitalistic gain.'

They were speeding along now up in the air. There were no roads, Arnold was astonished to note, from which he devined that all traffic here was done through the air.

They came to more parkland with a lot of people in the park. These people seemed to be walking about and they had paths just through the park. 'So they can stroll more easily, Arnold,' said one of his guides. 'We use walking as a pleasure and as a means of getting to places slowly so we only have pathways where we can practise pleasurable walking by the side of a river or lake, or in a park. Normally we go by controlled levitation as we are doing now.'

'But who are all these people?' asked Arnold. 'I have a most uneasy feeling that I—well, I seem to recognise some of them. It's perfectly absurd, of course, perfectly preposterous, it just is not possible that I know any of them or they know me, but I have a distinct and very uncanny feeling that I have seen them before. Who are they?'

The two guides looked about them and said, 'Oh, THEM! Well, that one over there talking to a big man was known on Earth as Leonardo da Vinci and he is talking to the one known on Earth as Winston Churchill. Over there—' pointing to another group—'you will find Aristotle who on Earth in days long gone was known as the Father of Medicine. He had a hard time getting up here because it was held that instead of being the Father of Medicine he delayed the progress of medicine for many, many years.'

'Oh, how is that then?' asked Arnold looking toward the group.

'Well, you see, Aristotle was claimed to know everything there was to know about medicine and about the human body and it was therefore a crime against such a great person to try to investigate further, and so a law was passed making it an absolute death-punishable crime to dissect a body or to make research into anatomical things because in doing so there would be insult to Aristotle. And that delayed progress in medicine for hundreds and hundreds of years.'

'Does everyone come up here?' asked Arnold. 'There seem to be not many people about if that is the case.'

'Oh no, no, no, of course they don't all come up here. Remember the old saying about many are chosen but few succeed. Many fall by the wayside. Up here there is a small number of people of very advanced mentality or spirituality. They are here for a special purpose, the purpose being to try to advance the progress of humanity on Earth.'

Arnold looked very gloomy. He had a terribly uneasy, guilty feeling. Then he said humbly, 'I think a mistake has been made, you know. I am just a poor monk, I have never aspired to be anything else, and if you say there are people of superior mentality or spirituality here then I must be here under false pretences.'

The two guides smiled at him and said, 'People of good spirituality usually misjudge themselves. You have passed the necessary tests and your psyche has been examined in very great detail, that is why you are here.'

They sped on, leaving behind the pleasure grounds, going up into what in another plane Arnold would have called a high country. He found that with his improving spiritual sight and fifth dimensional insight it would have been impossible for him to explain to anyone else what was happening. Before they came down to a landing in a very special city he had one further question: 'Tell me, do any people of the Earth plane ever come here and then return to the Earth plane?' he asked.

'Yes, under very special circumstances, very special people who have been chosen to go down there in the first place come up for a time to be, let us say, briefed on how things were at this time and to be given fresh information as to what they should tell people on Earth.'

They swooped down, three together as if tied together with invisible bonds, and Arnold entered into a fresh phase of existence, one which would be beyond the understanding of humans to comprehend or to believe.

THE OLD AUTHOR'S DREAM

The Old Author dreamed a dream, and this is the way he dreamed that dream. He was sitting propped up in his old hospital bed with the little typewriter on his lap. You know that typewriter? Canary yellow, given to him by his old friend Hy Mendelson, a nice light little thing which had quite a merry clack to it when used properly.

Miss Cleopatra reclined sedately by his side. She was dreaming of whatever Lady Siamese Cats dream of when they are full of food, when they are warm and comfortable. Miss Cleo, not to be too polite about the matter, was snoring like an old trombone, if trombones DO snore. But the clack of the typewriter inexpertly pounded was boring and monotonous, the hum of traffic outside was like the hum of bees harvesting in a field of flowers in the summer.

The Old Author had terrible backache. It felt like broken firewood pressing into the flesh and pinching the nerves. He could not move because he was paraplegic, you know—lacking the use of two legs. And, anyway, to have moved would have meant that Miss Cleopatra would have her beautiful dream disturbed, and a beautiful little cat like Miss Cleo would always have beautiful dreams and they should NOT be disturbed. But eventually the pain dulled and the typing slowed, and at last with a touch of asperity in his tone the Old Author said, 'Get out of my way, typewriter, I'm sick of the sight of you.' And with that he slid it onto a table at the side of the bed. Snuggling back as best he could he closed his eyes, and according to later reports from two biased people HE snored as well, a raucous, thrumming, rasping snore, so he was told. But, anyway, he snored, and as he snored he must have been asleep.

Many pictures formed before his eyes in the dream. He dreamed that he was floating above the streets and he knew that he was in his astral form but he thought, 'Oh my goodness, I hope I have my pyjamas on!' because so many people when they astral travel forget that according to civilised convention little pieces of cloth should at least cover certain areas of one's anatomy.

The Old Author floated along and then froze into sudden immobility. There was a two-seater car coming along and the old term 'hell for leather' would be suitable in this instance. It was an open two-seater car, one of those fast English things like an Austin-Healey or a Triumph or something like that, but it was fairly beetling along the road and the driver, a young woman, was not paying any attention at all, her long hair was streaming out behind her and every so often she took a dab at her forehead to wipe away the hair which was obscuring her view. So it was that at the very moment when her right hand was raised to sweep back the obscuring hair a car—a heavy old clunker of a car— came out from an intersection and stopped dead in her path!

There was one awful BONK and the rending of metal, the sound, in fact, was very much like when you crush a match box in your hands. The old clunker was pushed several feet along the road. A man got out of the driver's seat, bent over, and was heartily sick in the road with shock. His face looked a pale puce with fright—if you know what pale puce is. If you do not know what that colour is—well, he looked seasick or airsick or, in this case, carsick.

Sightseers with staring eyes and slack jaws appeared from everywhere. Rubbernecks peered out of windows, and small boys came scooting around corners yelling to their colleagues to come and look at the 'beautiful accident.'

A man rushed away to phone the police, and soon there was that cacophony which indicated that the police and an ambulance were coming to pick up the remains, and there were some remains! First the police car skidded to a stop, and then in this neck-and-neck race the ambulance skidded to a stop. Two policemen jumped out, and two ambulance men jumped out of their vehicle. They converged on the two cars.

There was heaving and shoving and many shouts. A policeman dashed back into his car and grabbed the microphone bawling mightily for a tow-truck. He was shouting so loud that it was hardly necessary to use a radio, it seemed that anyone in the city could have heard.

Soon from the far end of the street there came a flashing amber light, and a tow-truck came roaring along the wrong way down a one-way street. But that was all right, they do such things in moments of crisis. The tow-truck made a nice turn in the road and backed up to the wreckage. Quickly the little car, whatever it was, Austin-Healey, Triumph, or something, was towed back a few feet. As it came to a stop the body of the young woman dropped to the ground. She was still faintly quivering with the last manifestations of her ebbing life.

The Old Author floated above making an astral sound which might be interpreted as, 'Tsk! tsk!' Then he looked anew because above the now almost entirely dead body of the young woman a cloud was forming. And then the silver cord connecting the astral body and the physical body thinned and parted, and the Old Author saw that it was the exact replica of the young woman's body. He went to move after her shouting, 'Hey miss, hey miss, you forgot your knickers!' But then he remembered that young ladies nowadays did not seem to wear knickers, they wore briefies or panties or pantyhose or something else like that, and he reflected that one could not, after all, run after a young woman telling her she had lost her pantyhose, her bra, and all that. Then he remembered that he was paraplegic—in the excitement he forgot that he was not paraplegic in the astral. So the young woman drifted off up into the realms above.

Down in the wreckage men were pushing and shoving and scraping up what could have been a couple of bottles of ketchup or raspberry jam. The Fire Department truck came along and they connected up their apparatus and hosed down the road, hosed down the blood and the gore and the petrol—gasoline on the North American Continent.

There was gabble, gabble, gabble, and still more gabble, and the Old Author got tired of looking at that. Tinpot cars going back to tinpot collections. No, he looked upwards just in time to see the young woman's posterior being obscured by a cloud. He followed.

It was quite a good way, he thought, to spend a little time on a hot summer afternoon. So, having much experience of astral travel, he swept upwards and upwards and ever upwards until he outstripped (sorry, no pun intended!) the young woman and got 'there' before her.

She was dead to the flesh, and she was alive to the 'Other Side', and it was always interesting to the Old Author to see newcomers approaching the metaphorical Pearly Gates. So he entered the realm of what some people call the 'Other Side' and yet others call Purgatory but which in reality was merely what one should call a receiving station. He stood by the side of a road, and suddenly the young woman popped up straight through the centre of the road, she popped up a few feet in the air and then sank back to ground level.

A man appeared from somewhere and called to her, 'New Arrival?' The young woman looked at him disdainfully and turned her head away. Then the man called after her, 'Hey miss, how about your clothes?' The young woman looked down at herself with horror and turned a very fetching shade of pink. It was a good blush, it extended all over her ample form, back and front, top, bottom and sides. She looked at the man and then she looked at the Old Author—yes, he was a man too!—and then she broke into a run, her feet pounding on the smooth road.

She hurried along and then approached a fork in the road. For a moment she stopped and then she muttered to herself, 'No, I won't take the right fork because right is the side of the conservatives, I'd better take the left, I might end up with some good socialists.' And so she galloped on down the left road. She did not know that both led to the same place like the old song in the Scottish Highlands where 'You take the high road and I'll take the low, and I'll be in Scotland afore you.' So the two roads were just an experiment so that the recording angel (he liked to be called that) would have some idea of the type of person he was going to meet.

The young woman slowed to a trot, and slowed still more to a walk. The Old Author, being wise in the ways of the astral, just floated along behind her, he was enjoying the scenery, all of it. Then the young woman stopped. In front of her were some shimmering gates, or they seemed to her to be gates because she had been preconditioned to believe in heaven and hell, Pearly Gates, etc. She stopped and a nice old angel came out, opened the Gates, and said, 'Do you want to come in, miss?' She looked at him and snarled, 'Don't you call me "miss" my man, I'm "Ms." and don't you forget it.' The nice old angel smiled and said, 'Oh, so you are one of THOSE, eh? I thought you were a miss because you are missing your clothes, you know.' The young woman looked down again and blushed anew, and the old angel chuckled in his long beard and said, 'Now, don't you be nervous of me, young lady, or should it be lady/man, because I've seen them all, backways, frontways, and everything else. You just come in, the Recording Angel is expecting you.' He opened the Gates a bit more and she entered, and then he shut them behind her with quite a clang, an unnecessary clang the Old Author thought as he floated in above the Gates. But the old angel—she knew it was an angel because he was wearing a nice bathrobe and his wings stuck out from his shoulders and flapped feebly as he walked—but, anyway, the old angel led her along a little way and opened a door saying, 'You go in there, go straight along that corridor and you will find the Recording Angel sitting in the hall at the far end. You'd better be nice to him, now, don't be too sneering and don't be too Mssing or he'll mark you down for the nether regions, and what he says is final.'

He turned away and nearly bumped into the Old Author

who said, 'Hi, Pop, so you've got another one here, eh? Let's go in together and watch the fun.'

The Guardian of the Gateway said, 'Yes, business has been a bit dull this morning, been so many righteous people coming by I got tired of letting them in. I'll come in with you and we'll watch the fun. The others can wait a bit.'

So together the Angel of the Portal of Death and the Old Author walked arm-in-arm down the corridor, and in the big hall at the end they sat down together on astral seats as they watched the young woman, her behind twitching nervously, walk up to the Recording Angel.

The Recording Angel was a short fat man and his wings did not fit too well because they clattered a lot as he talked, it was much the same as an old woman—when she talks her teeth clatter and nearly fall out. Well, the Recording Angel was like that, every time he moved his wings twitched and, to make the matter even worse, the top sides of the wings kept on nearly knocking off his halo. With some astonishment the young woman saw that the halo was in fact held on with strips of sellotape. She sniffed hard, things were very peculiar, she thought, but just then the Recording Angel looked at her face—he had been looking at everything else first—and he asked, 'Date of death? Where d'you die? Where did your mother die? And where's your father now, heaven or hell?'

The young woman sniffed and sniffed. She was becoming frightfully embarrassed by all this, the way people were looking at her, and anyway some of the pollen from the flowers in the Heavenly Fields weren't half tickling her nostrils. Suddenly she gave one terrific sneeze and nearly blew the Recording Angel's halo off. 'Oh pardon,' she said in embarrassment, 'I always sneeze like that when I smell strange odours.'

The Angel of the Portal of Death did a wheezy chuckle, and said, 'Oh yes, him you know,' jerking a thumb at the Recording Angel, 'is a bit of a stinker. We get a lot of people sneezing when they get a niff of him.'

The Recording Angel looked at the papers before him and muttered, 'Oh yes, date of death, date of this, date of that. Well, we don't want that, I've asked the questions but if the young woman should give me the information I should be the rest of the day filling out forms, this red tape, you know—' Suddenly he looked again at the young woman's face and said, 'Say, did you bring up any spare fag ends? I could do with a smoke and it's a very strange thing but when people come up here first they always throw away their cigarette ends. They are a lot better off down in the hellish quarters because so many smoke there, anyway, before they're finished.'

The young woman shook her head in increasing amazement, indicating that no, she hadn't any cigarettes or anything else smokeable. So the Recording Angel grunted and said, 'Where d'you die? Did you have a good undertaker?' he fiddled about among his papers and picked out a card which read, 'I. Digsem, Buryemall Unlimited. Undertaking our specialty. Cremations a convenience.' 'There,' he said, 'that's where you should have been fixed up, we get a lot of customers from there and we always know just fine how well they've been treated because we look at their scars.'

The young woman was just standing there, and in the end she looked down and let out a shriek of rage: 'Look!' she screamed, 'You've got me down on that form as "Miss." I'm not miss, I'm Ms. I demand that you alter it now, I won't have this discrimination.' She fumed and fumed, and she went red all over. It was easy to see where she went red because she had no clothes on, so she went red all over and stamped her feet with temper. The Recording Angel made soothing noises and said, 'Whoa, whoa, steady there, now, steady. You know where you are, don't you?' Then he pursed his lips and made that sound known as a raspberry before saying, 'Well, miss—we don't acknowledge Ms. here —you have already decided where you are going to go because any Womens Lib person or any media person is denied the Heavenly experience. Instead they go down to the hellish fields. So there you are, lass, pick up your feet again and keep moving them forward. You'd better get down, I'll phone Old Nick now and say you're on the way down. Be sure you give him my kind regards in person because we've got a thing going to see who can take most patients from the other. He wins this one fair and square because you're a Libber!' He turned away and reached for his wastepaper basket. Then, scrumpling up her form, he put it in and carefully straightened up his desk and got out a fresh set of papers.

The young woman looked about her uncertainly and then turned to the Old Author saying, 'Aren't they most unhelpful here? There's such a lot of discrimination. I shall certainly complain when I meet the Top Brass, but how do I get to the hellish regions from here?'

The Old Author looked at her and thought what a pity she had to go to hell, they would certainly give her a roasting there with her bad temper and her 'smart Alecess' attitude. But then he said, 'It doesn't matter which way you go, all roads lead to hell, you know, except one and that's the one you've missed. So just start going down that road, you'll find you are going downhill fast.'

The young woman snorted and said, 'Well! Aren't you going to open the door for me? You call yourself a gent?'

The Old Author and the Guardian of the Portal of Death looked at her in astonishment, and the Guardian said, 'But you are one of these liberated people, if we open the door for you you will say that we are denigrating you and not giving you free rein to your rights, one of which is that you can open the blasted doors yourself!' The Guardian turned with a snort and bustled off to do his duties at the Gates because someone was trying to get in and rattling the bars.

'Come along, you,' said the Old Author, 'I'll show you the way, I've got quite a few friends down there, and of course an even greater number of enemies. But be careful when you get down there because about fifty percent of the population are ex-media people and they are not very popular. Come on, let's go.'

Together they walked down a road and the path seemed quite endless to the young woman who suddenly turned to the Old Author and said, 'But don't they have a rapid transit system here at all?'

'Oh no, no,' said the Old Author, 'you don't need a rapid

transit system here because everybody is going to hell as fast as they can go. Just look down at the people on Earth now,' and he nudged her to look over the edge of the road and there, to her astonishment, she found she was looking down to the people of Earth. The Old Author continued, 'Look at that man down there, sitting behind his big desk, I'm sure he is a publisher's editor or something, or possibly—' he stopped a moment and fingered his beard before going on, then, 'Yes, yes, I know exactly what it is,' he said excitedly, 'that one down there is an authors' agent. When you get down to the nether regions you might fork out a shovelful of hot coal and drop it on him. It will serve him as "coals of fire." '

Then they turned a curve in the road and before them were the Gates of Hell glowing blood-red and shooting off sparks in the murkiness. As the two came down the path towards the Gates the young woman saw a really hot devil grab his trident and a pair of asbestos gloves. Quickly putting on the gloves he reached for the handle of the Gates and swung them back, smoking and sending out showers of sparks. 'Come along, ducks,' he said to the young woman, 'we have been waiting for you, just come in to our party. We know how to deal with young women like you, we'll soon teach you that you are a woman and not just a libber. We'll teach you that you are a sex symbol okay.' He turned and pushed the young woman in front of him, and quite gently put the prongs of his trident to her posterior. She leapt up into the air with an eldritch screech, her feet pumping and running before she hit the ground again. The devil Gate Keeper turned to the Old Author and said, 'No, no, old fellow, you can't come in here, you had your hellish time on the world. Now we'll give some of your persecutors and detractors a bit of a roasting. You go back and stir up some more trouble, we want some more victims here for shovelling coal and carrying out the clinkers. Begone with you, do!'

So the young woman disappeared from the Old Author's dream. She disappears from our pages as well, and we can only surmise, perhaps lewdly or lustily, at the fate of such a young woman with curves in the right places and bumps in the right places condemned to such a beautifully hellish atmosphere, although she herself would have admitted she was not quite good enough for the heavenly atmosphere.

So the Old Author wandered up the path again keeping his eyes open and his ears open for the sights and sounds which made up such a large amount of the life of the hellish part of the Other Side. As he gazed about he saw behind him the inferno. Great gouts of flame shot up into the sky, and things which looked like fireballs—those things which are such a feature of firework displays. Then there were showers and showers of bright sparks going up describing a parabola and coming down again. Every so often there came hoots, shouts, and screams, and the whole area was of a ruddy hue which was most unpleasant. The Old Author turned away and as he did so there came the clatter of the red hot door opening, and shouts of, 'Author! Author!' A hellish crew (what a pity they were not a heavenly horde!) came pouring out of the open gates and rushed up the slope yelling, 'Author! Author!'

The old man sighed fit to bust the stitches out of his pants—if he had had any on—and turned back. At this point it might be as well, because of the lady readers, to make it clear that although he had no pants on he did have on the appropriate robe so the ladies can go on looking at the print.

There was a lot of beckoning, gesticulating, shouts and all the rest of it as the Author went down the hill again and sat on a bench from which he rose hurriedly because of the heat. From the gates a very large man with a pair of well-polished horns emerged. He had a tail with a barb on the end, and the tail had a very attractive blue bow on it. I suppose the blue was as a contrast to the prevalent red of the atmosphere. He came out and greeted the Old Author saying, 'I could do with you here, you know, I could do with you here in hell and I sure would offer you a very good job. How about it, eh?'

The Old Author looked about, and then he replied, 'I

don't know about that, this is sure one hell of a dump, you know.'

The Lord Satan looked even more satanic and picked his teeth with a splinter from some old coffin which he had happened to trip over on his way out. As he picked his teeth the wood charred and gave off tiny sparks as old rotten wood will. Some of the sparks fell in the direction of the Old Author, who fell even more quickly out of their way.

Satan said, 'You write a hellish lot, Old Man, that's what I want. I really could do with you and I have a lot to offer you, you know. What do you want? Dames or dolls, or whatever you call them? Small boys? No, don't vomit here, it'll make an awful stink with the press if you do. Or what else do you want?'

Well, the Old Author was feeling a bit vomitous at the thought of the small boys being offered, but then he thought of the dames or dolls, broads or what-have-you, and that didn't seem very attractive either. After all, everyone knows what trouble women can make——

'I'll tell you what!' said the devil with a gleam in his eye, 'I know what you would like! How about a bunch of liberated females and then you could teach them that this liberation is a stupid thing indeed. Yes, I can give you any number of these ladies, some of them are awful people, too. Just say the word and you shall have as many as you want.'

The Old Author scowled and said, 'No, I don't want any liberated women. Send them away as far as you can, keep them out of my way.'

The devil laughed out loud and he had a real devilish gleam in his eye as he shouted, 'I know, I know! How about a few media people, you really could have a hell of a time with them. You could let them write some hot words and then you could make them eat them. Yes, that would be the thing to fetch you in, have your fun with the media, they've had their fun with you. How about it, Old Man, eh?'

The Old Author shook his head once again. 'No, no, I don't want anything to do with those sub-humans, I regard media people as definitely evil, and they should be your handmaidens or handmen, or whatever you like to call them. Don't let me get near them, I don't like them. I would even like to strike an extra match under their boiling pot or whatever you do with them.'

The devil sat down on a fresh spot and steam rose alarmingly from his rump. He crossed one leg over the other and his tail swished with the intensity of his thought. Suddenly he jumped to his feet with a scream of triumph: 'I know, I know!' he shouted. 'How about having a nice yacht, or, as you have always been interested in paddleboats, how about having a nice paddleboat all on your own? You can have a hellish mixed crew and you can have a hell of a time going around in the hot lakes and all the rest of it. You can have the Red Sea as your playground. It's red with human blood, you know, you'll like it, hot blood tastes really good.'

The Old Author looked disdainfully down and said, 'Devil, you don't seem to know much. Don't you realise that if I had a paddleboat I would be in hot water because the Red Sea of human blood is just about boiling. Isn't that hot water?'

The devil laughed and said, 'You are making mountains out of molehills, or should it be molehills out of mountains. Anyway, what's your beef? Of course, down here the beef would be well cooked. But anyway, what IS your beef? You've been in hot water all your life, haven't you? I should have thought you would have grown accustomed to it by now!'

The Old Author fiddled about in the hot sand with his feet, drew patterns, and the devil looked down and screeched with pain as he spied various religious symbols such as the Tibetan Wheel of Life, etc. He screeched with pain and hopped up and down, and by accident he got one hoof on the symbol and up he went in the air with a whoosh, disappearing right over the red hot gates. When last seen he was flying in the direction of the Red Sea of human blood.

The Old Author was so astonished that he sat down on the bench again, and rose a great deal quicker than the devil had because that seat was hot, and hotter now that the devil had sat on it. But he dusted off his smouldering robe and decided that this was the time to get out of it, hell was no place for him. So once again he moved on up the hill away from the pit. This time he moved a darn sight faster.

At the top of the hill he met a guardian of the pits who greeted him affably and said, 'Hi, cock, haven't seen many coming this away, they're usually going thataway. You must have been too good to be let in.' Then he looked at the Old Author and said, 'Oh, yea man, I recognise you, you sure are some cat, you write them Rampa books, don't you? Well, you're no friend of ours, you've kept many a bad soul from coming to us. You be on your way, man, we don't want any truck with you, off you go.' And then, before the Old Author could get going, the guardian called to him saying, 'Wait a minute, wait a minute, I've got something to show you.' And he pointed to some strange device standing beside him, and he said, 'Now, look through that, you'll get a good picture of hell. It's interesting. You'll see all manner of stockades. We've got publishers in one, agents in another, media people in another, and over there to the left we have liberationists. Next door to them we have a special stockade for old Etonians, and, do you know, they don't fraternise a bit, no. But come and look for yourself.'

The Old Author approached gingerly and then changed his mind in a hurry at the amount of heat coming out of the eye pieces. Without another word he turned and made his way up the hill.

At the top he saw again the Pearly Gates. The Guardian of the Pearly Gates was just moving out to close and padlock them for the night. He waved, and said, 'Hiya, bud, did you like it in hell?'

The Old Author waved back and answered with a shout, 'No, there's too much of a hellish atmosphere down there.'

The Guardian of the Pearly Gates called back and said, 'It's worse here in our heavenly atmosphere, we've got to mind our "p's" and "q's." We mustn't say a bad word, if we do we have to go down to the pit and stick our tongue

173

on a hot plate there. I should go back and write another book if I were you.'

And that is what the Old Author did.

He moved along wondering what else he should look at, should he see the Fountain of Pearls or the Pavement of Gold? But as he was thinking that he heard a loud 'clang' somewhere. It sounded like glassware being clattered together. Then he felt a sudden pain, and he jumped back to awareness to hear a voice saying, 'Come on, come on, it's time for your injection.' And as he looked up there was an ugly great hypodermic needle coming down to poke him in the rump. The voice said, 'What, you writing again about the afterlife?'

'No,' said the Old Author, 'I am writing the last of this book, and these are the last words in this book.'

Rampa's Tranquilliser Touch-Stones

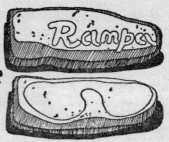

You are interested in the Higher Sciences or you would not be reading this book. Have you considered how your tranquillity can be nourished by a Rampa-Touch-Stone? On page 123 in *Wisdom of the Ancients* you can read about these Touch-Stones. They are available with simple instructions

AN INSTRUCTION RECORD ON MEDITATION

A large number of people wrote to Lobsang Rampa demanding a record about Meditation, so at last he has made the only special, fully authentic recording by him. Tells you how to meditate, shows you how easy it is, places peace, harmony and inner contentment within YOUR reach. A. Touch-Stones Ltd. can supply this 12″ record AND THE TRANQUILLISER TOUCH STONE ANYWHERE at the prices below AIRMAIL FREE.

Price List

	Record	Tranquilliser Touch-Stones	
Australia	7.00	4.20	dollars
Austria	120	100	schillings
Belgium	260	230	francs
Canada	7.50	5	dollars
Denmark	40	30	kroner
France	30	20	francs
Great Britain	2.00	1.85	pounds
Germany	17	11	deutsche marks
Holland	17.50	11	guilders
Nigeria	7.50	5	naira
Norway	36	24	kroner
S. Africa	5.50	3.60	rand
Spain	400	270	pesetas
Sweden	28	19	kroner
Switzerland	15.50	12	francs
U.S.A.	7.50	5.00	dollars
All other places	3.00	2.00	£
All other places	7.50	5.00	dollars

A TOUCH-STONES LTD.
33 Ashby Road
Loughborough
Leicestershire LE11 3AA
England

A SELECTED LIST OF PSYCHIC, MYSTIC AND OCCULT BOOKS THAT APPEAR IN CORGI

WHILE EVERY EFFORT IS MADE TO KEEP PRICES LOW IT IS SOMETIMES NECESSARY TO INCREASE PRICES AT SHORT NOTICE. CORGI BOOKS RESERVE THE RIGHT TO SHOW AND CHARGE NEW RETAIL PRICES ON COVERS WHICH MAY DIFFER FROM THOSE ADVERTISED IN THE TEXT OR ELSEWHERE.

THE PRICES SHEWN BELOW WERE CORRECT AT THE TIME OF GOING TO PRESS (FEB '78)

☐	09471 4	MYSTERIES FROM FORGOTTEN WORLDS	*Charles Berlitz*	65p
☐	09392 0	THE MYSTERIOUS UNKNOWN	*Robert Charroux*	85p
☐	09828 0	THE PROPHECIES OF NOSTRADAMUS	*Erika Cheetham*	95p
☐	09556 7	THE SPACESHIPS OF EZEKIAL	*J. F. Blumrich*	60p
☐	08800 5	CHARIOTS OF THE GODS	*Erich von Daniken*	85p
☐	09083 2	RETURN TO THE STARS	*Erich von Daniken*	85p
☐	09689 X	GOLD OF THE GODS	*Erich von Daniken*	85p
☐	10073 0	IN SEARCH OF ANCIENT GODS	*Erich von Daniken*	75p
☐	10371 3	MIRACLES OF THE GODS	*Erich van Daniken*	85p
☐	09853 1	FAR MEMORY	*Joan Grant*	60p
☐	09430 7	THE UFO EXPERIENCE	*J. Allen Hynek*	65p
☐	09556 7	IN SEARCH OF ANCIENT MYSTERIES		
			Alan and Sally Landsburg	50p
☐	10416 7	I BELIEVE	*T. Lobsang Rampa*	65p
☐	10087 0	AS IT WAS!	*T. Lobsang Rampa*	65p
☐	08880 3	THE THIRTEENTH CANDLE	*T. Lobsang Rampa*	70p
☐	08765 3	THE HERMIT	*T. Lobsang Rampa*	70p
☐	08611 8	FEEDING THE FLAME	*T. Lobsang Rampa*	65p
☐	08408 5	LIVING WITH THE LAMA	*T. Lobsang Rampa*	65p
☐	07652 X	CHAPTERS OF LIFE	*T. Lobsang Rampa*	75p
☐	10189 3	THE SAFFRON ROBE	*T. Lobsang Rampa*	75p
☐	09138 3	YOU – FOREVER	*T. Lobsang Rampa*	70p
☐	10628 3	DOCTOR FROM LHASA	*T. Lobsang Rampa*	80p
☐	09834 5	THE THIRD EYE	*T. Lobsang Rampa*	75p
☐	09390 4	CANDLELIGHT	*T. Lobsang Rampa*	75p

All these books are available at your bookshop or newsagent, or can be ordered direct from the publisher. Just tick the titles you want and fill in the form below.

CORGI BOOKS, Cash Sales Department, P.O. Box 11, Falmouth, Cornwall.

Please send cheque or postal order, no currency.

U.K. send 22p for first book plus 10p per copy for each additional book ordered to a maximum charge of 82p to cover the cost of postage and packing.

B.F.P.O. and Eire allow 22p for first book plus 10p per copy for the next 6 books thereafter 4p per book.

Overseas Customers: Please allow 30p for the first book and 10p per copy for each additional book.

Name (Block letters) ....

ADDRESS ....

(FEB 78) ....